I Shall Use My Freedom Well

Josiah Henson
Fugitive Slave (1789-1883)

JULIET HAINES MOFFORD

TouchPoint Press

I SHALL USE MY FREEDOM WELL:
JOSIAH HENSON, FUGITIVE SLAVE (1789-1883)
By Juliet Haines Mofford
Published by TouchPoint Press
www.touchpointpress.com

ISBN-10: 1-946920-22-3
ISBN-13: 978-1-946920-22-5

TouchPoint Press books may be purchased in bulk or at
special discounts for sales promotions, gifts, fund-raising, or
educational purposes. For details, contact the Sales and
Distribution Staff: info@touchpointpress.com or via fax: 870-
200-6702.

Editor: Kimberly Coghlan
Cover Design: Colbie Myles, colbiemyles.com

First Edition

Printed in the United States of America

Dedication

This book is dedicated to my four Grand-Girls:
Sarah, Emily, Juno, and Athena, for inviting me to
share my passion for history with you.

Contents

Acknowledgments

With sincere appreciation to Kimberly Coghlan of Coghlan Professional Writing Services for her patience and expertise. And to my first editor, Zoe Chamberlain-Suarez, a million thanks.

And for helping me get the details just right, many thanks to Steven Cook, Executive Director of Josiah Henson Historic Site, Ontario Heritage Trust, located at 29251 Uncle Tom's Road, Dresden, Ontario, Canada N0P 1M0.

Chapter One - Haunting Memories

The natural tendency of slavery is to convert the master into a tyrant and the slave into the cringing, treacherous, false, and thieving victim of tyranny.

Josiah Henson was born into slavery, an institution that designated him, *a thing* or piece of property belonging to his mother's master, Doctor Josiah McPherson. When she gave birth to him on the fifteenth of June, 1789, she was working for McPherson's neighbor, Francis Newman, near Port Tobacco, Charles County, Maryland. Newman owned the newborn's father and had hired her from the doctor temporarily.

Josiah McPherson not only gave the baby boy his own first name, he added the surname Henson in honor of an uncle who had been a soldier in the Revolutionary War.

Something happened a few years later that Josiah Henson would spend the rest of his life struggling to forget. Yet no matter how hard he tried the images of Papa's punishment and his terrible cries of pain flashed forever through his head. Indeed, the first chapter in Josiah Henson's history was unbearably sad.

Master Newman's overseer attacked his mother, and her screams brought Josiah's father racing from the fields. Finding his wife struggling to escape the overseer's clutches, he sprang upon him like an enraged tiger.

'My father would have killed the man for assaulting her, had Mama not warned him off,' Henson later wrote. Papa fled into the woods, hiding out for days, only venturing into some cabin at night in search of food. Hunger and fear of the slavers' hounds finally made Papa turn himself in.'

Even slaves from neighboring plantations were forced to witness his father's punishment for their own 'moral improvement.' Every slave knew the penalty for striking a white man: one hundred lashes, applied fifty at a time so as not to kill or permanently damage the master's precious property. Papa's lashes were laid on by a powerful blacksmith named Hewes.

It seemed to Josiah he could still hear Newman's command, "Strip the shirt off his black back!" as they forced Papa face down across a bench. The cat o' nine tails was a large rope of many strands with a knot tied at the end of each strand. As it tore into his lacerated flesh, Papa's cries grew weaker until they turned into soft moans.

Small as he was, Josiah understood his father was being hurt. Josiah and his five older brothers and sisters cupped hands over their ears and squeezed their eyes shut, but they could not erase Papa's screams of agony. Those screams would haunt Josiah and give him nightmares as long as he lived. Nor could he ever forget how frightened he felt. Young as he was, Josiah resolved this would never happen to him.

One of Newman's slaves threw a bucket of salt water across the torn flesh on Papa's back, then pulled him upright and pushed him against a wooden post. Mama had already taken Josiah and her other five children back to the slave quarters when they heard Papa's bloodcurdling scream followed by an eerie silence. The overseer had nailed his father's right ear to the whipping post and severed it from his head as the surrounding crowd cheered.

"That's what he gets for attacking a white man!" someone hollered.

"That'll show the black scoundrel!" another man called out. Several slaves expressed sympathy, but the majority seemed to consider Papa's punishment just.

Nor would Josiah ever be able to make himself forget all the blood when they carried Papa into the slave quarters. Standing in a circle with his brothers and sisters, the small boy watched their mother treat Papa's lacerated flesh with salves and heard his moans as she tenderly cared for him through the following days and nights. The children listened as the two people they most

3

loved in the world wept in each other's arms. Mama coaxed down Papa's fury, warning him against taking revenge or running away. They all understood something had happened that was so bad it was going to change things forever. The flesh wounds on their father's back eventually healed into scabs, then turned to scars, but Papa's spirit could not be mended.

"Used to be, your father was a right jovial fella," she told them. "A good-humored and light-hearted sort he was. When he played his banjo, he brought fun to every gathering. Why, your papa was always the ringleader, merry-making at corn-huskings and Christmastime. At such times he would play all night long—everyone dancing to the music he made." Josiah later remembered the sadness in his mother's eyes when he'd asked why the banjo now lay upon the shelf covered in dust.

"Your father is a changed man," she said. "Defeated and without hope now. Seems nothing can be done to make the poor man happy again." Josiah would always remember the day he saw Papa take his banjo off the shelf, look at it closely, and then, with a snarl, pull the strings from it one by one. Finally, he threw the instrument against the wall with such force that it smashed into pieces. Like his banjo, Papa was a broken man—consumed by anger and hatred. He no longer picked up Josiah and his brothers and sisters, riding them in turns upon his shoulders. He seemed to have forgotten how to play and simply sat around brooding. Mama had been able to heal his wounds but not his heart.

One day, the master's overseer appeared at the door to fetch Josiah's father and drag him into a wagon. They soon learned that Francis Newman had sold their father south into Alabama, and Papa disappeared from their lives forever. Mama wept for days, but no one ever heard from him again and never knew whether he was dead or alive.

A practicing physician who was too fond of whiskey, Doctor McPherson was gentler than most slave masters. He believed that slaves who were well treated performed their work better, so he seldom ordered his slaves whipped. Although they all missed Papa, Josiah's family was reasonably satisfied with life on McPherson's estate. The doctor was especially fond of his namesake and made a pet of Josiah. However, before the boy turned six, calamity struck, altering life forever.

One morning Josiah McPherson's body was discovered lying face down in shallow water. Riding home after an evening of drinking with friends at the local tavern, he apparently slipped off his horse, tumbled into the creek, and drowned in water less than a foot deep.

The most dangerous time for any slave was when their master died or experienced serious debt. Following Doctor McPherson's sudden death, his property had to be sold off to settle his debts with the proceeds divided among his creditors. Of course, the doctor's property included his slaves, since they were a valuable part of all he owned. Slaves were moveable property and had no rights over their own children, so Josiah's family went to auction to settle their master's debts.

Years later, Josiah could still shut his eyes and recreate that horrible day. He remembered being lifted onto the big wagon and placed on Mama's lap. Slaves of all ages were crowded into the wagon, and Josiah recalled feeling scared because so many of them were weeping.

"Where we goin', Mama?" Josiah asked. "Where dey cartin' us off to?"

The wagon finally halted before a crowd of people. Everyone seemed to be talking and pointing at once.

"We 'bout to be put on the auction block," Josiah's oldest brother explained. And they saw white folks pointing at the black men and women lined up on the platform. Some of these well-dressed white men were forcing black peoples' mouths open to examine their teeth while others were turning bare-chested black fellows this way and that, prodding their muscles.

Josiah soon came to understand that excited crowds such as this one consisted of slave owners, auctioneers, potential buyers, along with curious onlookers. Mama's three boys and three girls were torn from her arms one by one and marched up on the auction block to be sold to the highest bidder. As the auctioneer called 'SOLD' and each one of Josiah's brothers and sisters was led away by a new owner, Mama's wails followed them. And with each cry of agony, the two white men standing on either side of her gripped her arms tightly to prevent her from running after her children. At the time, Josiah did not understand this meant he would break all ties with his brothers and sisters—that he would likely never again see them. Yet, young as he was, Josiah felt as if 'iron entered my soul that terrible day.'

"Lookie here! A prime example of a healthy woman!" the auctioneer hollered to the crowd assembled around the stand. Mama let go of Josiah's hand as she mounted the steps onto the platform. "This gal's already proven herself a top-notch breeder. An' she still in the prime o' life!" The man cupped Mama's face in his hand, turned it from side to side, and forced her mouth open. "Got herself a fine set of teeth, too!"

Isaac Riley was the highest bidder and rose to claim his new property. Riley was a blacksmith and one of the largest landowners in Montgomery County, Maryland, having inherited over 400 acres of farmland from his father and aunts, along with three tobacco houses and twenty slaves.

Then it was Josiah's turn. A white man picked him up and set him on the stage.

"Folks, jes look at this sweet little pick-a-ninny!" shouted the auctioneer, pushing Josiah to the front of the stage. "A playmate for yer own son, eh? An' anyone kin see he gonna grow up to be a mighty strong buck!"

The bidding for him was still underway when Josiah heard his mother's desperate screams. "Don't take my baby," Mama wailed, pushing her way through the crowd. "Oh please, spare me one child!" She wept uncontrollably.

She fell at Isaac Riley's feet, clinging to her new master's knees.

"I beg of you, Master, buy my boy too! If you have a heart, spare me this baby!"

Riley looked down at her with disgust and shook his head. "What use is a small boy to me? Nothing but another mouth to feed! I've no need of him."

"He be no trouble," Mama begged Riley. "He well-behaved and healthy! Oh please, Master, buy my little boy!"

Showing no pity, Isaac Riley reached out a clenched fist and gave Josiah's mother several brutal blows. Mama's groans mingled with the sobs of a broken heart. As she continued to plead, Mama's new master thrust out one leg and gave her a violent kick, and she crawled away from Riley's reach.

"Lord Jesus, my husband sent far south to Alabama. My children sold off who knows where," she wailed. "How long must I suffer?" The scene would remain etched in Josiah's memory. It was 'a lifelong lesson in the cruelty of slavery that made humans heartless.'

"That little fella's cheap enough," Josiah heard a man say. "He's small now, but I wager he'll soon be big enough to serve customers at my tavern."

Adam Robb was his name, and he managed an ordinary not far from Riley's farm. Josiah soon found himself hoisted onto Robb's horse in front of this new master and taken away from Mama.

'The iron entered my soul that day,' Henson remembered years later. For without a word, Master Robb deposited him in the slave quarters where some forty others were asleep on bug-infested straw and piles of old rags. Josiah thought he would never be able to stop crying. Robb's slaves came in and out of the shanty over the next few days, but no one paid him any attention except to tell him to quit his crying.

Neglected, aching with hunger, pining with loneliness, and desperate for his mother, Josiah took sick. By the time someone took notice, Josiah was running a high fever.

"Well, you sure turned out to be a waste of money," Adam Robb said crossly. "Best I get rid o' you right quick! Don't wanna a dead pick-a-ninny on my hands!" He'd made a bad bargain and wanted his money back.

Isaac Riley agreed to take the sick boy off the tavern keeper's hands and reimburse him by having Robb's horses shoed at the blacksmith shop he owned. The two men agreed that should the slave child die, no money would be owed. Soon Josiah, weak and feverish, found himself hoisted upon a horse in front of an overseer and delivered to the Riley farm.

"Mama!" Josiah shouted, suddenly much better and sliding off the horse before it had halted. He raced into the slave cabin. "They brought me back to you." His mother had no words for her youngest child, only hugs and tears of joy.

Chapter Two - A Model Slave

Children like Josiah Henson went to sleep on the floor any place they found to lie down in their master's slave quarters. Snow blew in through the cracks of their hovel in winter and when it rained the dirt floor turned to mud. A dozen or so men and women slept on piles of straw and old rags without beds or other furniture. Small children went naked while the older ones wore itchy tow cloth shirts reaching to their ankles or loose pantaloons held up by drawstrings. A single blanket, along with jackets and wool caps, was doled out for winter, usually along with woolen socks or slippers.

Josiah's first job was to carry water buckets to field hands and to hold the horse plough between rows of corn and other plants at weeding times.

"Water!" Josiah shouted as loud he could to all the slaves at work in Master Riley's fields. "Quench yer thirst here!" He would suddenly be surrounded by men, women, and children, their faces dripping sweat.

"Canna do that," Josiah reminded any slaves who lifted the full gourd dipper over their heads, tipping it so the cool water flowed over them.

When Josiah hoisted the yoke across his shoulders again, the wooden buckets were empty and his load light.

Josiah was growing fast and always seemed to be hungry. His mouth was frequently dry as cotton, and his belly rumbled as he worked.

Breakfast came with the noon bell after laboring since daylight. It was nearly always cornmeal mush, occasionally with a bite of bacon or slab of salt herring. Buttermilk was a special treat. The second meal of the day arrived when work was done, though a third was provided during the height of harvest season.

'Though slavery did its best to make me wretched, we enjoyed jolly times on holidays: Christmas dances and eggnog before old massa's door and extra meat,' Henson later recalled. 'Midnight visits to apple orchards and first-rate tricks to dodge work. The God who makes the pup and kitten play, the bird sing, and the fish leap, was the author in me of many a light-hearted hour.'

When Josiah grew taller and somewhat older, he was put in charge of Master's Riley's saddle horse. He enjoyed this job and soon talked to the animal like a trusted friend. Later, a farm tool was thrust into Josiah's hands, and he joined the hoe gang for six straight days of 'weary toil under the blazing sun.' Whether the task was hoeing, mowing, or reaping, he was the first one in the field, determined to surpass those of his own age, and for that matter, any age.

Josiah was not always in Master Riley's favor. Indeed, when he was thirteen, he nearly lost his life due to an attempt at learning to read.

Among William Bell's regular duties was to deliver the Riley children by wagon to their school some five miles away and to pick them up in the afternoon. William, a slave belonging to Lewis Bell, had learned to read and spell by hearing his master's children discuss lessons as they rode to and fro. William told Josiah that if he bought a copy of *Webster's Speller* in a Washington shop, he would teach him to read. Josiah had already made himself some ink out of charcoal, and shaved a goose quill to match Master Riley's pen. He had begun to make scratches upon scraps of paper he found lying around. The first letters Josiah learned were I and R, which he'd seen stamped upon the butter he sold. He soon realized these letters stood for Isaac and Riley, the first and last names of his master.

If I gather some apples that fall from the trees in the orchard and sell them, Si reasoned, *I'll have enough money to purchase a speller.*

He was harnessing Riley's horse one morning when the animal suddenly became frisky and galloped off. As Josiah raced after him, he lost his hat, and the speller hidden inside dropped to the ground.

"What is that there, boy?"

"A spelling book, Master."

"And whose is it?"

"Mine, sir."

"Where did you get it?" Riley demanded.

"Bought it myself, Master, when I went to market for you."

"How much did it cost?"

"Eleven cents."

"And where did you get the money?"

"Sold some apples out of our orchard that I found lying on the ground," replied Josiah.

"*Our* orchard," exclaimed Riley. "I'll teach you to get apples from our orchard for such a vile purpose! Give me that at once!"

When Si stooped to pick up his book, he spotted Riley's cane coming down on him.

"I said pick up that book!" Riley raised his cane high and brought it down hard across Josiah's head and back, beating him until his eyes became swollen and he lost consciousness.

It was some time before Josiah was able to work again. He had a scar on his head from that day, and he did not open another book until he was forty-two years old and had escaped the Land of Slavery.

"Oh, so you wanted to become a fine gentleman, did you?" Riley sneered once Josiah was back at work. "Africans ain't supposed to read. Any white man who'd teach an African to read ain't fit to own a slave. Learnin' spoils slaves—if a slave learns to read and write it makes him useless to remain a slave."

"Yes, Master." Josiah nodded.

"Meddle with another book—let me catch you carrying any book again, an' I'll knock out yer brains!'

Lewis Bell's slave, William, got sent south to Georgia for teaching other slaves to read. "We won't have our slaves nor our neighbors' slaves spoiled by that rascal again," Lewis Bell exclaimed.

****

By the time Josiah turned fifteen, everyone was calling him *Si* for short. He could now run faster and farther than anyone else, and few could compete with him either at work or at sport. Si was able to wrestle better and jump higher too, and he was aware that others, including his fellow slaves, often spoke of him as *a smart fellow*. Why, even Master Riley predicted he was going to accomplish great things when he became a man. Whenever Si overheard such talk, he couldn't help but feel proud, even though he knew most people believed it impossible for a slave to aim for success.

'Pride and ambition was as active in my soul as they likely ever were in the soul of the greatest soldier or statesman,' Henson wrote years later.

Si was determined to be a model slave. The fate of his father would not be his. Instead, he would out-hoe, out-reap, out-husk, and out-dance every other slave that Isaac Riley owned. He toiled extra hours to show his master what a good day's work he had done, hoping to win a few words of praise.

'One word of commendation from the petty despot

who ruled over us would set me up for a month,' Si later recalled. 'A smart slave understands how to master the master. The clever slave becomes skilled at telling the master whatever he wishes to hear.'

Josiah was not above stealing a stray pig or chicken now and then and carrying it deep into the forest where he would butcher, pluck it, and build a roasting fire. He then distributed these tasty treats and provided a feast for his fellow slaves, especially the older women and mothers with babies.

He became accustomed to running down a chicken in an out-of-the-way place to hide till dark and then carrying it to some poor, overworked black friend to whom it was food, luxury, and medicine for the good of those whom Riley was starving. Si did not think Master Riley would miss a few chickens from his flock nor even a sheep now and then. Si was held in high esteem by his colleagues for this.

'Since we were, all of us, hungry nearly all of the time, I esteemed this among the best of my deeds,' Henson said.

Although Isaac Riley was too hard-hearted to offer words of praise to any of his slaves, Si's efforts at being a model slave apparently had not gone unnoticed. When the young man was eighteen, he became more than just another field hand. Having caught his overseer stealing, Master Riley dismissed the fellow on the spot and promoted Si to the position, saving himself the expense of hiring another white superintendent. This privilege was given only to slaves who had gained their master's trust, and the new job filled Si with pride as well as the determination to do his best. And he was pleased that he seemed able to inspire his fellow slaves to work more cheerfully. He was also responsible for punishing any hands on the farm who were lazy or misbehaved. As overseer, Si soon doubled the yield produced on Master Riley's plantation.

****

Isaac Riley then appointed Josiah Henson to be his market man. Because Si was so reliable, his master regularly referred to him as 'my manager.' Si was confident he always got the best possible prices for Master Riley's produce. It was his responsibility to drive the ox wagon piled with bales of hay, oats, barley, and potatoes, along with fruit from Riley's orchards, some fifteen miles to Georgetown and Washington City. This wagon had to be loaded the night before market day with the oxen hitched up to leave the plantation around midnight in order to arrive by morning.

Si's customers hailed from all over the area, and he was convinced that speaking with these strangers greatly improved his ability with the English language. He also knew to select the best butter for the best families in the capital city and took pride in delivering it directly to their homes. Si was eager to imitate people he respected as gentlemen, and by listening attentively to how others spoke, he learned to speak properly. He even gained a basic practical knowledge of law from hearing lawyers discuss their cases. This skill would eventually enable Josiah to recognize and protect his own legal rights.

Si kept strict and honest accounts for Master Riley. He reckoned every dollar in sales of all the goods entrusted to him. It remained a mystery to Josiah how he gained the knowledge of figures necessary to sell all that produce from Riley's four farms in the Washington markets since he never studied arithmetic. Indeed, Josiah continually calculated any possible opportunity to increase his value in his master's eyes and thus improve his condition, though Riley seldom seemed to notice. Perhaps Isaac Riley was incapable of doing such business transactions himself and could not express gratitude for his slave's competence and marketing ability.

On trips to the capital city, Henson often observed coffles or lines of slaves in chains being led to some slave pen or auction. He would never forget the despair and fear he read in those faces. Josiah got to know a few free black men in Washington. Some he spoke with even showed Si their free papers and explained how they had managed to earn enough money to buy their own freedom.

Among Si's new friends was a Georgetown baker named John McKenny. This baker was a Methodist minister who regularly bought Master Riley's grain. He claimed to be an enemy of slavery and proudly declared that he employed no slaves in his business. John McKenny often preached at a nearby chapel. He told Si that his sermons were meant for the slave as well as the master and for the poor as well as for the rich.

Chapter Three - Tavern Brawl

Truth be told, Si's master was frequently in his cups and disabled by drink. Isaac Riley spent nearly every Saturday evening in the taverns, gambling at cards, betting on fighting cocks or horse races, and consuming large amounts of whiskey. It was Si's job to push his stout master into the buggy or back in his saddle and lead the inebriated man home, strolling through the darkness and mud beside the horse.

Si was waiting outside for his master on the front stoop of the tavern one night when he heard a scuffle inside and Riley's cries for help. Tavern quarrels were common, and Si opened the door to yet another bar room brawl. His master was a bruiser and could usually hold his own, but this time he was cornered by a dozen men striking at him with fists, crockery, chairs, and anything handy. Tankards were flying through the air, and broken glass already covered the floor. Pistols were being fired and dirks drawn. Si knew it was his duty to plunge in, drag his drunken master out of the fight, and see him safely home. As he elbowed his way through the crowd of white men, he heard his master shout, "That's it, Si! Pitch in now an' save me!"

Si could clearly see that his master was crazed with drink and rage. He would have to do for Riley what the man could not do for himself. It should be as easy as hauling a sack of corn, but that particular evening, Riley had been engaged in an especially nasty quarrel with Bryce Litton, the overseer at a neighboring plantation.

"Help me," Master Riley whined in desperation as Si confronted the tangled pile of inebriated men. Bryce Litton was immediately upon him, and they were locked together, wrestling viciously. Si, younger and stronger, quickly had the overseer pinned to the floor beneath his knee. Litton blamed Si for the fall rather than the whiskey and immediately swore vengeance.

"You'll pay for this, boy," Litton snapped. "Jes' you watch out! No black fella dares make a fool of me!"

Si finally managed to get Riley out of the tavern, push him into the wagon, and drive him home. He had nearly forgotten the incident until the following week when Master Riley sent him on an errand. To save time, he led the horse on a shortcut through the woods. Riding along the path, Si glimpsed Bryce Litton standing in the field with three slaves. When Si returned half an hour later, the overseer was seated on the fence. Sensing no particular problem, Si rode on. Suddenly, Litton jumped off the fence, and two black slaves appeared from behind the bushes where they had been hiding, while a third jumped off the fence, landing right behind him. Si was now surrounded by enemies determined to do him harm.

"Git off yer horse," ordered Litton, grabbing the bridle.

"Why should I?"

"To take such a flogging as you never had in yer life, ya black scoundrel!"

"What am I to be flogged for?"

"Not a word outa yer mouth," the overseer snapped. "But light at once and take off yer jacket."

Si dismounted and removed his jacket.

"Now off with yer shirt!" Litton raised his arm to strike Si but spooked Si's horse instead. The frightened animal reared, broke away from the group of men, and galloped off, leaving Si without any means of escape. The four men knocked him to the ground and were immediately all over him with hard blows. Si fought back as best he could. Kicking with his heavy shoe, he knocked out one fellow's front teeth and sent him crawling away, howling. Litton hit Si again and again with a large stick across the head and all over his body, drawing blood but not quite knocking him senseless.

Then Litton threw the stick aside and seized a fence rail about six feet long with which he began to strike Si over and over with all his strength. In his attempt to ward off these blows, Si's right arm was broken. He was back on the ground where all four men continued to beat him, breaking both his shoulder blades. Blood gushed from

Si's mouth, and he was in excruciating pain.

"Don't murder him, Mister Litton," all three slaves begged. "If'n ya kill 'im, we all gonna hang."

"Aye, that's so," the overseer nodded. Then, standing over Si, Litton said with a snarl, "Now ye'll remember what it means ta strike a white man."

Si lay on the ground helpless and barely conscious. With every torturous breath he took, he felt and heard pieces of his shoulder blades grate against one another. Meanwhile, Si's horse had returned to the house without a rider in the saddle, which raised alarm so that Si was soon found and carried home.

No physician was called to dress Si's wounds or set his broken bones, for the master did not waste money on doctors. Instead, Riley's sister, Patty, splintered Si's broken arm and bound up his back as best she could, but it was five months before he was able to return to work. The first day he tried to plough, a hard knock against a stone shattered one shoulder blade all over again, causing him even more agony than before. Si had been maimed for life and was never again able to raise his arms above his head.

Isaac Riley swore out a warrant for Bryce Litton's arrest, intending to prosecute the overseer for abusing and maiming his prize property. However, when the case went before the magistrate, Litton claimed Henson 'had sassed him and attacked him first and that the three slaves were only protecting their overseer.' The judge concluded that Litton had merely acted in self-defense, and a black fellow as strong as Josiah Henson would likely have killed Bryce Litton on the road had not those other slaves been standing nearby to save him. The overseer was acquitted, and since a black man's word was inadmissible in any court of law, Isaac Riley was ordered to pay all the court fees. At least Si's master had the satisfaction of calling Overseer Litton a liar and a scoundrel although that ended up costing him an additional fine. In spite of the injuries that crippled him for life, Si maintained his position as Riley's chief overseer and market man.

Chapter Four - Conversion

Sometimes, returning home from the nation's capital, Si stopped by the chapel at Newport Mill, about four miles from the Riley farm, to hear his friend, John McKenny, preach. Perhaps it was the music that also drew Si there, for jubilant singing filled the little wooden building and seemed to rock its very foundation. Si listened and learned and felt as if he had been awakened to a new understanding of life.

Slaves were generally barred from entering meetinghouses to attend worship services, but Si's mother urged her son to coax Master Riley for permission to attend Sabbath services. Finally, Riley reluctantly gave Si permission to go but warned the young slave what would happen to him if he failed to return to the plantation immediately afterwards.

One day, on his way home, the eighteen year old suddenly found himself kneeling on the ground asking for enlightenment. Si's 'heart had been opened to the

God of Love, the same being who had created playful kittens, birds that sang and fish that swam. I was filled with a special light that made me feel quite merry. Somehow, life seemed to have suddenly become easier. Even my loyalty to Master Riley seemed strengthened through conversion.'

Si was determined to find out more about this Jesus fellow who cared about the plight of the poor and had the power to make sick folks well again. Why, Jesus had even been flogged like Si's own father.

During Sunday services, there also a lot of talk about a book called The Bible. Si longed to know more about this book that seemed so important, but he did not know how to read. However, he began to pray with his fellow slaves, all of them hoping for some spiritual conversion that meant awakening to a new life and easing their daily difficulties. Master Riley didn't voice much opposition because he saw that Si's preaching was calming to his slaves and seemed to make them more contented.

It was at revival meetings in the chapel that Si met and fell in love with Charlotte who belonged to a neighboring family. She was well taught for a slave and considered an especially good cook. Si claimed it was Charlotte's singing of spiritual songs that first won his heart. The more he and Charlotte became acquainted, the deeper their affection for each other grew.

Since they were both but pieces of property, their marriage had no legal significance, yet slave couples could form mutual agreements. In a traditional ceremony, cheered on by Master Riley's slaves, as well as those from neighboring estates, Charlotte and Josiah jumped the broom when Josiah was twenty-two. Most slave owners encouraged their slaves to marry and bear lots of children since that increased their work force. Of course, slave masters had the legal right to claim each child as soon as it entered the world.

Charlotte and Josiah moved into a small log house with a dirt floor along with ten other men, women, and children. There was no furniture, and their beds were made of straw and rags, thrown in the corner, and boxed in with boards with a single blanket as their only covering. The couple's favorite way of sleeping was on a plank with their heads raised upon an old, folded jacket. When the wind whistled outside and the cold wind blew in through the cracks, they lay with their feet warmed before the fire. Charlotte raised vegetables in the truck-patch, the small piece of ground assigned them, and it wasn't long before they welcomed their first child, calling him Tom.

When Master Riley was forty-five, he took an eighteen-year-old bride named Mathilda, who brought some property to their marriage, including her own slaves. Her younger brother, Francis, also moved to the farm since Master Riley was now his legal guardian. The new Mistress Riley was known for being thrifty, so their marriage failed to add any comforts to daily life. Si considered Mathilda Riley miserly and difficult to please, but he became genuinely fond of Francis. Frank, as he was known, was a growing boy who was harshly treated by his new stepfather and always seemed to be hungry.

"There's never enough to eat around this place," Frank complained to Si and Charlotte whenever he showed up at the slave quarters. Young Frank knew they could easily be coaxed into sharing whatever they happened to have on hand.

Chapter Five – Issac Riley's Plan

One January day in 1825, Master Riley came to the slave quarters seeking Henson.

"You must help me, Si," he said on the verge of tears. "I am ruined. All is lost!" He explained that he had come out on the losing end of a recent lawsuit with his brother-in-law who had sued him for mismanagement and even dishonesty regarding some property given him in trust. And now he was in desperate financial straits. "I have nothing to offer my young wife to satisfy her needs, much less her wishes. I am here to beg your help." Si pitied the man. This poor, drinking, moaning creature was incapable of managing his own affairs.

"I am truly sorry for your misfortune, Master Riley, but what can I possibly do for you?"

"I have thought much on this matter and have managed to devise a plan that I think rather clever." Isaac Riley grinned, as if congratulating himself. "Everything depends on you, Si. It's up to you to save us all."

"Depends on me?" Si asked, baffled. "How can that be, Master? Whatever do you mean?"

"I've come up with a means of preventing you and all my other slaves from being sent up for sale. Before I explain, you must promise me you will do as I propose. I stand here before you, Si, pleading for your help."

"I am listening, Master." Riley knew Josiah Henson was sure to keep any promises he made.

"Before the sheriff has a chance to seize and repossess everything I own, you must run away with all my slaves to my brother Amos' plantation in Kentucky. You and your family will have to pack up and prepare to depart immediately. I'll provide you with a pass, but you must all slip away before my creditors arrive."

Si could not believe what he was hearing.

"I know I've abused you in the past, Si, but I didn't mean it. I raised you from a small boy. I made you my overseer. Promise you'll do this for me, boy," he whined tearfully. "Otherwise, it's to Georgia or Louisiana with all of you."

The thought of being sold south to those southern states—of having his family sold and scattered, likely forever, filled him with sheer terror. Si vowed to do all he could to save his master.

"But Master Riley," he said, hesitantly, "I have never traveled further than Washington City. Never been more than a day's journey from this farm. How will I ever find my way to Kentucky, much less take your other slaves there? Why, it must be a thousand miles distant!"

"Oh, it's easy enough for a smart fellow such as yourself." Riley slapped Si on the back. "You could find your way anywhere in the world! You are the only man to lead my slaves to Kentucky. I'll show you a map and tell you how to find my brother's plantation. Do as I ask—no—as I beg of you," Master Riley pleaded. "'Tis the only means I have of being saved from financial disaster; the only way to keep my slaves off the auction block!" Riley saw Si shudder at those words and then added, "And I expect to follow you there within a few months as I am planning to reestablish myself in Kentucky—give myself a new start there, you see."

It was obvious that the slave-owner was now dependent upon his slave. Riley was placing faith in him, and Josiah would like to save the poor fellow from financial ruin if he possibly could. After all, this man had raised him from boyhood.

"All right, Master Riley." Si nodded. "I will do as you ask. You can count on me to deliver your slaves to Kentucky."

Charlotte was reluctant until Si explained that should she stay behind, she would most assuredly be sold away from him and their two little boys.

However, Josiah's mother was not able to make the trip. She had grown too old and feeble for anyone to want to buy her anyway. They both wept as Si said goodbye, fearful they may never again see each other.

Josiah and his family departed in the middle of frigid February with eighteen slaves. Master Riley provided Si with a special pass authorizing him to lead his slaves all the way to Kentucky.

Riley also gave him money to cover travel costs and a horse-drawn wagon along with ample provisions for the trip that included bacon, oats, and root vegetables. The women and younger children rode in the wagon while the men, trudging alongside, got to ride only when they became too tired or lame. The group followed the new National Road across Virginia, through Harper's Ferry, and into the mountains of western Virginia to Wheeling, spending nights in roadside taverns that accepted black travelers. Si sold the horse and wagon in Wheeling as Riley had told him to do and bought a yawl for the voyage down the Ohio River. These slaves were accustomed to following Henson's directions on Master Riley's estate, so they did not question his leadership now.

Chapter Six - Cincinnati

With so many people heading west in search of land and new opportunities, Cincinnati had become a boomtown with plenty of jobs available. Passing along the Ohio River, Josiah Henson and his charges were greeted by curious folks who kept reminding them they were no longer slaves but free men and women.

"'Tis folly to keep on goin' to Kentucky when you standin' right here in the free state of Ohio."

"Slaves you may be but slaves you no longer hafta be!"

Si could see that some in his charge became increasingly excited, but he was committed to honoring his sworn duty to Master Riley back in Maryland.

"Dis yer chance, people. Stay here where we all free," the strangers coaxed the group.

"Why you thinkin' to cross the river inta Kentucky where you be slaves again?"

"Yo' are fools not to light out for freedom!"

"Why think of travelin' to some new master when

you can be your own masters here?"

Si was torn. Here was the chance to liberate himself and his family from a life of bondage. He studied the faces of his fellow slaves and saw most were filled with the same hunger for freedom he felt. In his companions' faces, Si could read the same dream of liberty that had nurtured him for as long as he could remember. Freedom had been a constant motive and the object of his ambition from his earliest recollection. Yet Si intended to save every bit of money he was able to earn, and then pay Master Riley to obtain his freedom. Running away had never entered his mind. To Si, that seemed the same as stealing one's self. Every cent that Si could call his own had already been set aside with the purpose of buying liberty. Why, he'd already accumulated $40! Anyway, he had promised Master Riley he would deliver his property safely to his brother, hadn't he? And that brother was across the Ohio River in the slave state of Kentucky. He had been given a great responsibility. His master had put his trust in him and Si believed he must see it through.

Si already had a picture in his head of Amos Riley welcoming the group upon their arrival in Kentucky and the admiration and respect that would be his reward from both Riley brothers. Still, the thought of liberating all his companions and running off with Charlotte and their boys was mighty tempting.

"What do you think?" Si asked his wife. "Should I break the vow I made to Master Riley? Should we all break free here in Cincinnati?"

"If you do, my dear husband, you will never be able to live with yourself. Nor with me either," Charlotte replied. "I know it's a great temptation but would it truly mean freedom for us? I hear tell Cincinnati is filled with trackers hungry for profits from pursuing runaway slaves. And you know Master Riley and his brother would have the hounds on us all pretty quick!"

"That's so. I could not cherish our freedom nor that of our children, if won by breaking a solemn promise I made the master."

"You must do what you think best, Si," Charlotte said, "though I think you should give the others the chance for their own freedom while here. Let them decide their own destinies."

Later, Josiah addressed the entire group, presenting the options and reminding them that, as Isaac Riley's property, they were not necessarily safe—not even in this free state of Ohio.

Tempting though it was, every man and woman in Si's group decided to stick with him and trudge onward to Kentucky. Si ordered the boat pushed off the levee in spite of the shouts and curses from shore. The slaves under his leadership, accustomed as they all were to obeying orders, raised no objections or resistance.

They left Cincinnati and freedom behind before dark, each one seemingly realizing they had thrown away a rare opportunity. Although he and the other slaves had no way of knowing it at the time, this fateful decision would haunt Si the rest of his life.

Chapter Seven - Amos Riley's Plantation

It was mid-April when Josiah and his exhausted charges finally arrived at Amos Riley's plantation on Blackford's Creek in Daviess County, Kentucky, near Owensboro. Si saw at once that Amos was far more prosperous than his brother back in Maryland. This man had five farms located five miles south of the Ohio River and owned one hundred slaves, that number immediately enlarged by Si and his companions.

Conditions were a great deal better on Amos Riley's prosperous estate too. There was a welcome abundance of vittles. 'The sufficiency of food is important in everyone's life,' but perhaps, Si thought, even 'more so for the slave whose appetite is particularly stimulated by hard labor and whose mind is occupied with little else.'

Josiah Henson was appointed superintendent of Amos Riley's five farms. His family was assigned a cabin near the river where they could see across to the free state of Indiana. Six days each week, Si rode from farm to farm supervising the work of Riley's field slaves, and on Sundays, he preached. Si and Charlotte spent the next three years here, expecting their true master, Isaac Riley, to arrive any day.

Si enjoyed special privileges as Amos Riley's farm superintendent. For six days each week, he rode from farm to farm, managing workers, and on Sundays, he was usually allowed to attend religious services as well as go to camp meetings in the area. Occasionally, Si was even invited to preach, something that filled him with a renewed sense of purpose. Slaves were permitted to keep any pay they might earn on Sundays, their only day off.

Indeed, the dream of freedom so long in Si's heart at last seemed possible. He knew that somewhere very far off, there was a place without slavery—a place where all men, women and children were born free—a place where a man could own his own home and till his own land. A man couldn't call anything his own in this life when his body belonged to somebody else.

In the spring of 1828, Isaac Riley's slaves received terrible news. Their master would not be coming to Kentucky after all. His wife, Mathilda, refused to leave Maryland, so he would remain where he was. He was sending an agent to his brother Amos' plantation with instructions to sell every one of his slaves except for Josiah Henson and his family. As soon as they were all auctioned off, Josiah was instructed to return to Isaac

Riley's farm with all proceeds from this slave sale. Isaac Riley would need Si's help with the few acres he still had left in Maryland.

Josiah was haunted by regret. *Why did I not encourage them to stay in Cincinnati? They could have all been free*, he reproached himself. "I can never forgive myself for making the conditions of their lives worse," he told Charlotte. "Now they will be torn from their loved ones and sold off —and most likely sold south."

The demand for slave labor in the Deep South had increased thousand-fold with the economic boom in cotton and laws forbidding the importation of slaves from Africa. Slaves were now worth more than ever.

In keeping faith with my master, I betrayed my friends. They might have found freedom, but instead, I led them to the cruelest bondage of all. 'Tis I who doomed them to a life of misery. Tears flooded Si's eyes and splashed down his face as he relived the memory of his own mother's anguish when, one by one, her children were torn from her arms. Once more, he envisioned the auction block and seemed to hear Mama's screams as each one of his brothers and sisters was sold off. Now Si was forced to relive the grief he'd experienced as a small boy as Isaac Riley's eighteen pieces of human property got liquidated.

'My soul is pierced with bitter anguish,' he told Charlotte. 'I am tortured at the thought of having been instrumental in consigning so many of our fellow beings to the infernal bondage of slavery.'

"You cannot blame yourself, Si," his wife said, putting her arms around him. "You did what you thought best. You had no way of knowing it would end like this for these poor souls."

"Did what I thought best, you say," Si replied, bitterly. "Oh yes, I kept my promise to a heartless master—that's what I did! And I led my friends into a worse hell! For their loyalty to me —their trust in me, these poor folks are doomed to end their days in despair and bondage. How can I ever forgive myself, Charlotte?"

"You could not know things were going to turn out this way, dear husband," Charlotte said gently. "The real mistake you made was to put your faith in Isaac Riley."

****

In the summer of 1828, a dynamic Methodist circuit preacher arrived in the area. This clergyman expressed special interest in Si's potential as a minister, knowing he regularly attended services with enthusiasm and was working hard to develop his speaking skills.

"You're a fine preacher, Henson. You should be a free man," the parson told Si. "You have far too much natural ability to be confined to the sphere of slavery."

Si listened and learned. He carefully studied gestures employed by other preachers, and often, when he was alone in the woods or fields, he practiced speaking aloud. Before the year was out, he was admitted to the Conference of the Methodist Episcopal Church and received a certificate that permitted him to preach wherever invited. Si was more determined than ever to earn enough money to buy his freedom. He felt certain he could do it now.

Chapter Eight - The Cruel Conspiracy

Charlotte did not accompany Si back to Maryland that September since she had a new son to care for. Anyway, Si expected he would be back with them in Kentucky soon.

"I must not be known to have spoken to you on this subject," Amos Riley said before Josiah left, "but if you obtain my brother's consent when you get to Maryland, I will fix it so you can buy yourself."

Si carried a legal pass from Amos Riley with him along with a letter of recommendation from his Methodist minister friend permitting him to preach anywhere along the way to Maryland and thus earn cash after delivering sermons. In Cincinnati, he preached from three different pulpits, although the city brought back painful memories of what might have been for Isaac Riley's slaves when they were under his care. Si even attended the Annual Conference of Methodist Churches in Chillicothe with his friend and colleague,

MOFFORD

Hiram Wilson. By the time he left Ohio, he had $275 in his pocket along with a fine horse and a brand new suit of clothes. Even before Si purchased this stylish outfit, he found he was treated with respect by everyone he encountered. What a contrast this was compared to the days when he was simply known as *Riley's head nigger* and suffered physical abuse. Josiah Henson was now a man of dignity.

It was Christmastime when he arrived back at the plantation in Maryland and rode up to the main house. Isaac Riley greeted him warmly at first and then gasped in amazement at Si's appearance since this slave was dressed far better than his master ever was.

"Why, whatever have you been up to, Si?" Riley demanded. "Look at you! Haven't you become the gentleman though," he exclaimed, eyeing Si up and down. "I thought you'd be back much sooner," he added then. "Did ya think I wouldn't know you left my brother's place back in September?"

"Yes sir, Master Riley, but I did some preaching on my way here," Si replied proudly. "You see, sir, I am a real minister now."

Isaac Riley made no response but simply ignored Si's news. "Just hand over all the proceeds due from the sale of my slaves," he demanded. "I'll have your pass back too, boy, including that permission paper for you to return to Kentucky." He thrust out his hand, looking Si over again from head to toe. "I can see I'm gonna have to knock the gentleman out of you pretty damn quick.

You're still my slave, Henson, no matter how fancy ya get yourself decked out."

Si seemed to 'hear the old prison gate clang shut again as he reluctantly handed over his pass.'

"So this authorizes you to return to my brother Amos in Kentucky," Riley said, glancing over the paper. Then he summoned his wife who hurried to his side. "Mathilda dear, lock Si's pass away in the desk drawer at once," he told her before turning back to Si. "As for you, boy, get that horse fed and groomed in the stable, then bed down with the rest of the slaves. There's plenty work ahead for you tomorrow."

Si lay on the filthy earthen floor in his old slave quarters that night—so different than the accommodations he had enjoyed in Cincinnati. The other slaves sleeping around him now were strangers, having become Isaac Riley's property following his marriage to Mathilda. Si found sleeping difficult, for he sorely missed Charlotte and the boys. He wondered how soon he could get away from Isaac Riley and make his way back to them.

Si's mother had died during his stay in Kentucky so there was nothing to keep him here. It saddened him that he never got to tell Mama he had become a minister and had proven successful at holding folks' interest with sermons. How pleased she would have been to learn he was now a preacher.

Mathilda's younger brother, Master Frank, was still Si's good friend and was currently a businessman in

Washington. Isaac Riley had already departed for the local tavern the day Josiah left for the capital city, but the mistress was at home.

"I am off to visit your brother," he told Mathilda Riley. "But I must have my pass."

"Oh, everybody around here knows you, Si," she said, cheerfully. "You won't need a pass."

"I might meet a stranger who demands I show it," he replied. And to his relief, she fetched the document from the desk and presented it to him.

"I am very pleased to see you, old friend!" Frank greeted Si with enthusiasm. "And looking so handsome and finely dressed!"

During the day they spent together, Frank openly revealed the hatred he had always felt towards his stepfather.

"As my guardian, Isaac Riley cheated me out of property that was rightfully mine," he told Si. "And my sister always takes his side! I don't understand why she puts up with him."

Henson told Frank how eager he was to obtain his liberty and how he'd earned money towards buying it. "I have a good amount of hard cash saved up," he told his friend.

"If you wish, I would be willing to speak to my stepfather on your behalf," Frank offered. "Why, you've already paid the man a hundred times over with your many years of hard work and loyalty, Si. Just think how much money you saved the old skinflint on the prices you got for his produce at market."

That same week, Frank visited the Riley plantation on Henson's behalf, and Isaac Riley finally agreed to issue him manumission papers for $450 of which he was to pay $350. Si already had $250 saved from preaching so he sold his horse and new suit of clothes for another hundred dollars. He signed an I.O.U. for the remaining $100 and anxiously awaited the manumission papers, which finally reached his hands and were dated March 9, 1829.

Now he was ready to return to Kentucky and the family he so missed. "And what will you do with your freedom?" Riley asked, as Si prepared to depart. "Do you plan to show your manumission papers when you are stopped by authorities on your way to Kentucky?"

"Of course, sir."

"Ahh, I do hope you are aware of the danger," Riley warned. "You will likely meet slave hunters on the prowl who will think nothing of stealing those documents right out of your hands and ripping them up before your eyes. Then before you even know what's happened, you'll find yourself in chains and locked in prison—soon to be sold to cover your jail fees."

Master Riley's words gripped Si's heart which seemed to freeze inside his chest.

"Why not let me keep those valuable manumission documents safe for you?" Riley suggested. "Your regular pass will do just fine to get you back to Amos in Kentucky. Look here, I'll seal up your manumission

45

documents so that when you arrive, you'll have them safe and sound. Nobody would dare break a personal seal since that's against state law."

That seemed like sensible advice—even kindness on the part of his old master, so Si handed over the precious papers. He watched as Isaac Riley enclosed them in three different sized envelopes, carefully sealing each one with wax and his personal stamp. He then addressed the top envelope to Amos Riley, Daviess County, Kentucky.

****

Anxious to earn additional cash on his trip, Si accepted an invitation to preach in Alexandria, Virginia, then got arrested because he didn't first request the mayor's permission. Si suddenly found himself behind bars on a Saturday, sentenced to 39 lashes at the public whipping post on Monday, or pay the $25 fine because preaching to slaves was against the law. Fortunately, he was able to get a message to Frank, who hurried to the jail. Si gave Frank his watch, worth $45, which covered his fine and bail. However, before climbing into Frank's coach and leaving town, Si delivered a sermon to a group of black citizens gathered near the prison.

'I gave them one of my best sermons,' Si later said. 'I doubt they'd heard such a good one in a long time. As soon as I was finished, Frank quickly got me out of Alexandria.'

Si managed to earn additional money as a circuit preacher before boarding the boat from Wheeling,

Virginia down the Ohio River, but he got arrested and had to appear in court several more times before reaching Kentucky.

Fortunately, Si was released each time he showed the authorities his pass.

Amos Riley greeted Si warmly when he arrived. "Glad to have you back, Henson!" he said, and Si knew the man was genuinely grateful for his labor. "You're lookin' mighty good, boy! A sight for sore eyes. And I hear tell you made yourself some money preachin'."

Riley then brought up the topic of Si's freedom. "So how do you plan to raise the rest of the thousand dollars to pay my brother and myself?" he asked. "You realize you still owe us $650?"

Si's mouth dropped open in shock, and his heart pounded. Could the Riley brothers really have upped the price of his freedom? Had they dared to add another zero to the $100 I.O.U. he had already signed? He could not believe the two men would be this devious and play such a nasty trick on him.

"The price for my freedom was $450," Si replied firmly, trying hard to control his temper. "Neither you nor your brother ever quoted me a sum of $650."

"Oh, so you believed the price for your freedom was but a mere $450?" said Amos Riley, feigning ignorance. "Why, surely you recall, Henson, one thousand dollars was the price we all agreed upon for your freedom!"

Si could not believe his ears. These brothers had played a trick on him when he had served them both so faithfully all these years. Were they such villains that they would up the cost of manumission another six hundred and fifty dollars?

"'Tis true," Charlotte informed her husband tearfully. "I overheard Amos Riley reading a letter to his wife from Isaac in Maryland saying your price was one thousand dollars. It's good to hear you earned some cash preaching, Husband, but how will you ever manage to raise the rest?"

Josiah found it difficult to fathom such treachery and questioned his wife again about what she'd heard. Each brother would like to own Si if they could afford to, but they both would be just as happy to sell him and split the profit. He had been swindled and was struggling hard to control the rage that rose in him at this crass betrayal. These two brothers represented men without consciences. Si would like to confront Amos Riley, and if the man stuck to the revised price he quoted, Si 'was ready to land a tight fist upon the liar's white face.'

"Dear husband, you know better than most folks that striking a white man will only get you whipped and worse—a severed ear and the whole of your body sent south," Charlotte said, trying her best to calm him. "Better to consider something practical you might do instead."

Si knew his wife was right. He realized now the only evidence that he was a free man was what had passed between the two brothers. He and Charlotte shared a pot of tea as they discussed what might be done.

Si realized that his old master, Isaac Riley, had instructed Amos to keep his manumission papers until Josiah gave him the $650 they claimed he'd agreed to pay. The only witness was his friend, Frank, but he was many miles away in Washington City, and Si did not dare ask anyone else to contact Frank since any man capable of writing a letter around here was a slaveholder.

"My papers must never be surrendered to Amos Riley. I shall tell him I haven't seen them since Louisville," Si told Charlotte. "For all he knows, that thrice-sealed envelope is still at the bottom of my carpetbag. Or perhaps, I'll tell him the packet got lost or was stolen." And this was how Henson responded when Amos Riley asked for his manumission papers.

"Where are the documents now, boy? What became of your freedom papers?"

"Last time I recall seeing the packet was in Louisville, sir. There were no papers when I looked in my satchel."

"Hurry right back to the landing, Si!" Amos Riley demanded. "Most likely you dropped them when you got off the boat." Si returned to the anchored vessel with some of Amos Riley's other slaves so they might observe the search and then reported back that he had been unable to find the packet.

"Never mind," Riley shrugged. "Bad luck happens to everyone. 'Tis of no consequence. When you turn over all the money due, my brother will issue you another manumission paper from Maryland. You won't get such good treatment here in Kentucky as in Isaac's home state."

Josiah and Charlotte continued working for Amos Riley another year during which time Amos came to Si several times complaining because Isaac kept writing him desperate for money.

"You must come up with another installment towards the price of your liberty, Josiah," he said. "My poor brother, Isaac is in dire straits."

"Alas, Master Amos, I have nothing to give," said Si.

Chapter Nine -To New Orleans in a Flat Boat

"Make ready for your trip down to New Orleans," Amos Riley announced one morning to Si's surprise. "I expect you to depart tomorrow with my oldest son. You are to accompany Amos Junior down the river and assist him in disposing a load of cargo. You'll also be carrying produce from neighboring estates and selling whatever you can for the best prices possible along the way."

Master Riley described this as a routine trading voyage to the port of New Orleans, but the man's intent was immediately clear to Josiah. Amos Riley informed Si that he had already hired three other men to travel with Si and twenty-one year old Amos Junior. As they spoke, the flat boat was already being loaded with pigs, poultry, beef cattle, corn, and all manner of other farm products, along with provisions that the travelers would need on en route.

"Aye, Master Riley, I will prepare to leave at once."

Si replied obediently although he was actually gripped by fear. He took care not to let this show but clearly understood what the devious Riley brothers had in mind. With his brother in Maryland, Master Amos intended that after the flatboat arrived in New Orleans and the livestock, along with the rest of the cargo had been disposed of, Junior would put Josiah up for auction, and the Riley brothers would split the proceeds of his sale.

Si was going to have to devise some plan to outsmart these heartless slavers. He was not about to allow them to rob him of the future he had been dreaming of so long. As long as there was life left in him, he would cherish his hope for personal liberty. Si forced back the fury that was on the verge of erupting inside him.

'I stood ready then to plot like a fox and fight like a tiger,' Si later recounted. He vowed never to let the Riley brothers know he was aware of their conspiracy and this devious plan to trap him.

"Would you be so kind as to sew me a pocket?" he asked Charlotte that same morning.

"Whatever for, husband?"

"To hold my manumission documents," he replied. "I plan to put the envelope inside a piece of cloth and secure it around my waist. Those precious papers may be my only salvation from spending the remainder of my life in miserable servitude."

Charlotte and the boys accompanied Si to the landing, and as he hugged them and said his goodbyes, he feared it was for the last time. Although Charlotte did not say the words aloud, she also wondered if she would ever again see her husband. It was not the usual trepidation over storms, dangerous sand bars, shipwrecks, or getting smashed by some steamer plying the waters that filled Si with fear as he boarded the flatboat. No, it was fear for his very survival—'a life of enslavement that would doom all his hopes for liberty. It was the shipwreck of his soul.'

Though one of the fellows Master Riley hired was familiar with Mississippi travel and experienced at river trade, acted as captain, each man aboard took a turn at the helm. However, after several days on the river, the captain's eyes became inflamed and swollen, rendering him temporarily blind.

"Must be the loss of sight that comes from too long staring at the sun's reflection upon the river," the captain said. "Since you've stood by my side these past few days, Henson, I do believe you can man this boat. I've decided to put you in charge."

Before taking to his bunk below deck, the captain cautioned Josiah to avoid the treacherous sandbars and to steer clear of the rapid currents and fast-moving steamboats.

"Keep a man on watch all night, Henson," the captain urged. River robbers abound in these waters. If you don't stay awake, they're bold enough to row right alongside and plunder our cargo by dark."

Josiah Henson served as master of the vessel for the remainder of the voyage down the mighty Mississippi

River to New Orleans. They stopped in Vicksburg, Mississippi, and Si visited the plantation where some of his former companions, those slaves who formerly belonged to Isaac Riley, had been sold. It broke Si's heart to see what four years of work in this unhealthy climate under a brutal master had done to them all. Forced to toil half-naked under the burning sun in the mosquito and malaria-infested place, with cheeks hollow from starvation, they seemed to look forward to nothing but deliverance through death. Si was sick at heart seeing these wretched folks again, knowing he might have helped lead them all to liberty in Cincinnati. He 'felt nothing but woe and despair because what they were presently suffering was no fault but his own.'

One rainy night a few days sail from New Orleans, Si was alone on deck on watch, pacing to keep awake. His mind dwelt on the Riley brothers whose promises had turned to treachery. So this was how they planned to repay him for his many years of service? He needed to find some means of escape before he was put on the auction block since he could not survive more betrayal and enslavement.

Si felt 'abandoned and cast off by God. As he paced the deck to stay awake, he mused that if it was his fate to be sold into a life as short and miserable as the lives of his former colleagues now at Vicksburg, then why shouldn't he shorten the lives of these men delivering him to the same injustice? Si's anger was fueling him into a dangerous man.'

How difficult could it be to take over this vessel and shorten the lives of all four fellows aboard? They have no suspicion of me and are completely under my control at this time, he thought. It would be an easy task to kill them all while they are sleeping. Indeed, he would do the deed this very night. No moon was visible through the darkness now. Si saw neither lights that indicated other boats nearby nor any sign of steam ships as he gripped the steering wheel. I will prevent any further treachery against me, he told himself. He made up his mind to be rid of his companions and take whatever cash he could find, along with any provisions he could carry. Then he would scuttle the flatboat and make his escape north to freedom. Since they were just a few days short of New Orleans, he knew 'he had to strike now. He would not be an innocent lamb led stupidly to slaughter!'

Si crept noiselessly down the narrow stairs below deck. He spotted the axe mounted on the wall above the other tools and grabbed it. His four shipmates were snoring in the cabin. Si could make out Amos Junior's form and tiptoed to his side. He stood over the young man, running his fingers lightly across the sharp edge of the axe. He gripped the handle tightly and raised the axe as high as his weakened shoulders would permit in order to strike the fatal blow.

Commit murder? Whatever was he thinking? He had been thinking of this act as self-defense, but he was contemplating breaking God's holy commandment: *Thou Shalt Not Kill.* Take the life of this young man who had done him no harm and was only following his father's orders? Had the Riley brothers' conspiracy turned him into a savage beast? Si's hand still gripped the axe, but it was at his side now. He realized he had been thinking of murder as a means of saving his own life, but this was a heinous, capital crime that could only end with the gallows.

Chances are, I could never get away. They would surely hang me. A hunted criminal I would forever be. He thought of Charlotte and their boys whom he would never see again. I am a gospel minister, Si reminded himself. For many years, he had worked hard at self-improvement to earn this respected role. And a preacher is a man whose sermons are an attempt to teach others how to better live their own lives. He carefully set the axe back in its place on the wall and climbed the narrow steps up to the deck.

It was a beautiful night, and the stars shone brightly as Josiah wept aloud in gratitude that he had murdered no one. *Better to die a slave nursing some dream for freedom than to destroy another life,* he thought. When his shipmates cheerfully greeted him the following morning, Si could not help but wonder if they could read the shame and guilt on his face. Did these four white men know how close to death they had come last night?

Chapter Ten - New Orleans

It was mid-June when they dropped anchor in New Orleans, and the crowds that thronged this bustling city seemed to make the heat even more unbearable.

"Father said to find buyers for whatever's left of the cargo," Amos Junior reminded them. "Then we are supposed to sell the flatboat. After that, you three fellows are discharged," he informed the hired men. "I am glad your eyes show improvement," he then told the captain, "but you still need to see a doctor. Wouldn't want you to stay blind."

As Josiah joined the others unloading and hawking produce along the waterfront, he spotted several coffles, processions of slaves being transported in chains by burly men with whips. Si pictured himself among these human trains of misery. And delivering bushels of corn a few blocks away, he could hear the auctioneer's shouts.

"What am I offered for this fine, strong buck! The very field hand you need!"

"See this comely wench! Young and strong. She'll bear you plenty of slave babies!"

Soon it will be my turn, Si thought with a chill of terror. This was when he decided to confront young Amos directly. "Planning to put me up for sale here are you, sir?"

"I expect I am, Si," the young man replied with a deep sigh. "Father thinks I can get a real good price for you. Maybe some rich planter in need of a coachman or house servant will buy you. My orders are to dispose of you after we get rid of the boat. Then I'll head right home on the next steamer going my way." Amos Junior must have read the horror on Si's face, for he immediately added, "I'm right sorry, but those are my instructions. Doncha worry, Si, I'll find you a good master."

"Pray, do not sell me," Si pleaded, clinging to the young man as his mother had once done in the attempt to save her children from slavery. "Don't sell me away from my wife and children. Have I not served your family well through many years—your father and your uncle both? Why, you've known me since you were a baby."

"Aye, you've been a faithful servant to our family for as long as I can remember," young Riley agreed. "I hate to see you go, but I am bound to do as my father instructed. I have no choice in the matter."

Did this lad have any idea how close he'd come to losing his life on the boat? Would he ever know that for the grace of God, he would be lying in a pool of blood in his bunk, dead from an axe blow? Although Si knew he himself would likely soon be in chains, he could not help but feel glad that this young man yet lived. Indeed, Si was relieved to think all four men owed their lives to his conscience.

Several planters came aboard to examine Josiah while they were still unloading the flatboat. "He looks to be a smart enough fellow," Si heard one say.

"Aye, but see how his back is deformed?" the other man pointed out Si's shoulder blades. "Poor fella's broken bones ain't healed right."

"That won't prevent him from hard work. An' it'll surely lower his price!"

The prospective buyers then sent Si on a make-believe errand, coaxing him to hurry just so they might determine how fast he could run.

They make a study of me as if I were some dumb animal at a livestock show, Si thought bitterly, but he ran fast for them anyway. They might as well be buying a horse, he thought. To all white men, I am but a piece of property—a financial investment.

****

"Ohhh, these pains in my belly are killing me!" Amos' groaning woke Si before dawn on the very day he was scheduled to be sold. "Help me, Si," the young man moaned.

By breakfast time, it was clear Amos, Junior was very ill. For the rest of the day, he lay with his head in Si's lap, trembling with fever and pain.

"Do something to save me, Si. I'm too young to die."

A doctor was summoned to the inn where they were staying and immediately diagnosed his patient with river fever, a malady that was apparently quite common in these parts.

"Stick to me, Si! Get me back home as soon as you can," Amos Junior begged. "I don't want to die here! Pray help me."

Si was now this young man's only friend and likely the only person able to save his life. "I won't desert you, Master Amos," Si reassured the poor fellow who continued to suffer and refused to eat anything but a few teaspoons of gruel. Indeed, Junior seemed near death, and Si realized that should he die here, his body would simply be tossed in the river since he was not a resident of the City of New Orleans.

"Please don't leave me, Si," young Amos cried. "I am so sorry I was about to put you up for sale. Forgive me," he wept.

So his conscience troubles him, thought Si. Well, so does mine for I stood ready to kill the fellow as he slept on the flat boat.

By the time Josiah managed to get Amos Riley Junior carried by gurney aboard the steamship and settled in the special cabin reserved for sick passengers, the poor fellow could neither speak nor move his legs and arms. Si had packed the young man's trunk and collected all the proceeds from their trip to New Orleans. He carefully counted the money once again and clipped the receipts together to turn over to Master Riley in Kentucky. Although it briefly crossed his mind to keep some of the profits for himself, Si knew he'd likely be caught and punished for stealing.

The steamboat swung away from the levee and sailed swiftly with the mighty tide of the Mississippi away from this city of bondage. Si knew the trip back to Kentucky would take at least twelve days, but to his relief, Junior rallied somewhat during the trip.

"Stay with me, Si," he whined. "Don't leave me, not even for a minute!"

The young man's condition remained grave, and Si continually coaxed him to swallow fresh water to moisten his painfully sore throat. As promised, Si kept constant vigil by his bedside the entire trip home.

"I so regret I nearly sold you back there in New Orleans," Amos Junior told him when he was able to speak clearly again. "If it hadn't been for you, Si, I'd be dead."

It was the tenth of July when they arrived at the Riley estate, and since the young man was still unable to walk, Si summoned some slaves to carry him by litter in relay teams along the five miles from the landing to the house. No one was more surprised to see Josiah Henson standing at the front door of the great house than Amos Riley Senior.

"Young Amos fell dangerously ill with river fever," Si explained. "Your son suffered greatly and was at death's door, but he seems much better now."

"'Twas Si who saved my life," Amos Junior murmured, groggily. "Si stayed by my side and nursed me all throughout my illness."

It was not until mid-August that Amos Riley's eldest son was well enough to leave his bedchamber.

"I owe my life to Josiah," he told the family. "Had I sold him as you told me to do, Father, I would be a dead man now."

Though all the Rileys were grateful to have their son and brother safely home and recovered to full health, the fact the young man owed his life to Si seemed to make little difference to Master Amos. A few words of praise, then back to work. What he had done for his master's son only enhanced his market value. Such evidence of Si's loyalty and good sense was sure to increase his worth on the slave block.

Chapter Eleven - A Resolute Decision

Josiah Henson's mind was made up. He knew he could never trust the treacherous Riley brothers. To both masters, he remained mere property—a means to their selfish ends. It would be only a matter of time before they put him up for sale again. If Isaac Riley had only been honest enough to keep his part of the bargain, I would have stuck to my side and paid him all I promised to, thought Si. But his devious attempt to kidnap me after pocketing three-fourths of my market value absolves me from any obligation to pay him more.

Si began to formulate a definite escape plan for himself and his family. They would flee north all the way to Canada—that far-off place known as the Promised Land. Why, a slave was not even safe in the free states of this country anymore. He was well aware of the risk and knew it was even more precarious for a slave who fled in the company of children. He understood that the odds against reaching safe refuge in Canada were slim. And yet, Si was now prepared to risk everything, including his life and the lives of every member of his family. He had acted the part of 'good slave' all his life, and it had come to naught but betrayal by his white masters. He no longer dared trust anyone.

The idea of freedom was an obsession for Josiah now. Evenings, he meandered the path along the riverside and gazed across to Indiana, knowing that state would be the first leg on their long, precarious route.

"Oh no, Si," Charlotte objected when Si told her he'd finally made the decision to flee. "It's far too dangerous! We would never stand the chance of escaping with four youngsters."

"We'll plan our trip very carefully, dear wife," he reassured her. "I will carry the two little boys. Tom and Isaac are big enough to walk and help carry blankets and food."

"I won't go," Charlotte said stubbornly. "Master Riley will send hounds yelping after us and likely post one of those *WANTED* broadsides. We'll all be caught and made to suffer a hundred lashes or more! Give up this lame-brained idea, husband. Please, I beg you."

Josiah stubbornly refused to scrap his plan and spent weeks trying to persuade Charlotte to change her mind. His wife had never experienced a human flesh market where slaves were auctioned off to the highest bidders. She had never suffered the horror of having her family ripped apart as his own mother had.

Indeed, Charlotte was fortunate never to have been haunted by Si's memory of Mama's agonized screams.

Si knew better than to share his worse memory of Papa's torn flesh and bloody, severed ear with Charlotte, though he did tell her of the horrors he'd recently witnessed in Vicksburg. And he tried hard to convince his wife of the happiness they would share together safe from pursuit in the Land of Freedom.

"It is for our family that I refuse to give up this idea, my dear. Nobody's going to own our bodies anymore! You must know that the Riley brothers will sell us any chance they get," he reminded her. "'Tis only a matter of time 'til they do. Running is the only chance we have to stay together and keep our boys with us." He told her once again how his mother had been forced to suffer the sale of his brothers and sisters, never to see them again nor know where they were or if they yet lived. Si pleaded and argued with Charlotte, but she would not give in. Yet Josiah knew he must have his freedom, no matter the cost.

"We will all die in the wilderness," Charlotte wept. "Or else, they will hunt us down and whip every one of us to death."

"If you refuse to go, Charlotte, then I must leave without you," he finally told her. "I must chance an escape to Canada—the country without slavery." It would be a cruel trial for him to part with Charlotte, yet Si felt he no longer had any choice but to flee. "I will take our three oldest boys so that they may have their chance for liberty rather than grow up in captivity."

Charlotte cried herself to sleep every night for

weeks, but Si remained resolute. He yearned for her to join him, but if she would not, he was still set on leaving. Then one day, as he headed for the fields to work, she came running after his horse.

"Si! Wait," she called, summoning him to halt. He reined in the horse so she could catch up. "I *will* go with you, husband," Charlotte said.

Blessed relief! Si's tears mixed with Charlotte's as he hoisted her onto the saddle and held her in his arms. How could he have ever considered abandoning her and their baby? Si realized now that all the Hensons must share the life of liberty together or die trying.

****

Since Charlotte and Si had been living at Amos Riley's farm nearest the boat landing, that should make it easier to get away. The couple made careful preparations that included putting aside non-perishable food. Always clever with her needle, Charlotte fashioned a large knapsack of tow cloth with strong straps to go across Si's shoulders. He would carry the youngest boys who were just two and three years old. Each night, Si practiced trotting back and forth across the cabin with these two little ones tucked inside to get them accustomed to it. Of course, they considered 'ridin' horsie' with their daddy pure delight.

It was mid-September when Josiah announced that the time had come to depart. "Tie up your things in a sack," he told Charlotte and the older boys, "but keep in mind that we must travel light."

"We have to carry enough victuals for our growing boys," Charlotte insisted. "I've been putting food by. You know, dried apple rings, salt pork an' such."

"We'll leave Saturday night," Si told them. "That way, we won't be missed right away. If luck is with us, no one will notice us gone before Wednesday. The field hands will think I'm riding here an' there overseeing Riley's other farms like I always do."

Tom, the eldest boy, had been working as a house servant and sleeping in the main house, so Si rode there on Saturday afternoon.

"Will you permit Tom to come to his mother for the next few days, Master Amos?" Si politely requested. "Our boy's growing so fast, an' she needs to fit him for some new clothes she's sewing."

"Of course, Si. Tom can go along with you," Riley replied.

"Thank you, Master Amos. And good night," Josiah said with a respectful bow. Then he chuckled to himself, 'knowing how *long* a good night this one was going to be.'

****

The moon was not visible the night they left. Charlotte shushed the boys as they climbed into the small skiff. Si had already talked one of Riley's slaves into rowing them across the Ohio River.

"Will ya promise ta conceal my part in dis?" the slave anxiously asked Si, pulling the oars. "Should I be found out, 'twill be de end o' me. I'm a dead man if'n

67

y'all get caught."

"Swear to God, I will never give you up," Si replied, patting the man affectionately on the back.

"But den, y'll wouldn't be brought back alive anyway, wouldja?"

"Not if I can help it," Si replied.

"An' if'n ya do get caught, y'll neber reveal I had any part in dis business?"

"Never," Josiah reassured his friend. "Not even if they shoot me through like a sieve."

"Den I am easy," the oarsman said. "An' I wish y'all God speed! An' may God help ya," Riley's slave said as they climbed out of the skiff and onto the shores of southern Indiana.

It was their first step to freedom, and Si already felt he had already become his own master.

Chapter Twelve – Fugitive Family

"I'm hungry, Pa," Tom began complaining when they had walked just a few miles into Indiana.

They traveled by night when it was safest and rested most days hiding in thickets. They trudged cautiously and steadily through seemingly endless woods. After dark, they kept to the roads, hiding whenever some horseman or wagon appeared in the distance. Si's back steadily ached from the weight of his smallest sons, made more painful because of his badly knit shoulders. Would he really be strong enough to carry these two little boys some six hundred miles on his crooked back? How much could Charlotte and these children withstand? How long would these provisions last? Would they be able to find edible plants and wild berries in the woods? His family was depending on him. Could he prevent them from starving?

As Si doggedly put one foot in front of the other, he wondered how long he could last himself. He tried not to think how far it was to Canada. And how would he even know the way?

'We were thrown absolutely upon our own poor and small resources,' Henson later recalled, 'and had to rely on our own strength alone. We dared look to no one for help.'

Never mind, Si reassured himself. Cincinnati is our first destination. That's about a hundred fifty miles eastward, and some of the folks I met there on my earlier visit will surely offer a helping hand.

Unaccustomed to being in the forest, Charlotte begged Si to turn back whenever she heard strange sounds. Just the hoot of an owl could bring her to frightened tears, which in turn, alarmed the older boys.

"I'm sure that was a wolf I heard howling," she exclaimed. "Oh Si, please let's go back before it's too late. Maybe we haven't even been missed yet."

Occasionally, along the way, they discovered caves where they welcomed shelter and a chance to rest. The older boys seemed to complain of hunger constantly.

"My stomach hurts," whined their second son, Isaac. His family's cries of hunger and exhaustion grated on Si who found their discomfort so distressing.

He watched Charlotte nursing the baby and wondered if she would be able to get enough nourishment to sustain the needs of their smallest boy.

Charlotte rationed out some of the roasted corn, dried venison, and cheese, and they all shared nuts and berries gathered along the way.

"We kin' catch us some fish, Pa," suggested Tom. "I know Mama has a needle and some string in her pocket. It'd be no trouble findin' a stick for a pole."

"Good idea, Tom, but save that thought for later," Si replied. "We need to make haste to reach Cincinnati."

Josiah had heard that Quakers living in the Richmond, Indiana area, were abolitionists by their religious faith and thus, sympathetic to fugitives, yet he feared trusting any one.

Charlotte and the older boys complained of the dark but didn't dare build a fire in case slave catchers were on their trail.

"I've never liked nights when there's no moon overhead," Charlotte said.

"Can't see where I'm going, Pa," Tom complained.

"Dunno what I might be steppin' on," Isaac whined.

"Mos' likely some deadly poisonous snake," Tom teased his younger brother, yet his voice seemed to shake with fear.

"How will we know how to find Canada, Papa?" Isaac wanted to know. "It's too foggy to see any Big Dipper"

"Just keep looking for the North Star," replied Si. "It's the one star that doesn't move. Least that's what those other fugitives told me when I was in Cincinnati a few years back." *Blessed be God for setting that North Star in the heavens*, Si thought as he trekked along, for it announced where his family's salvation lay.

"I think it's called the pole star," Tom said. "'cause

71

it marks a fixed point."

"Can't see it," Isaac whined. "Too dark."

"Then feel for moss growing on the trees," Tom told his younger brother. "Moss grows on the north side of trees."

"The North Star will soon reappear," Si reassured the boys. "And we'll follow it through these woods and across streams and fields, 'for it will guide our feet along the way of hope.'"

They tripped over tree roots and got scratched by brambles. With skinned shins and bloodied knees, they stumbled over sharp rocks. Twigs and thorn bushes marked their faces, and the sticky mud came up to their knees, yet the Hensons trudged on.

"My feet hurt somethin' terrible," Tom complained.

"You should see my blisters," Isaac fretted. "They bleedin' bad."

Si stopped walking to look down at both boys' bare feet and nearly wept when he saw how cracked and bloody they were.

"I hungreee," Josiah, Si's third son, cried from inside the knapsack on his back.

"Quit your whining," Si warned the little ones reaching back to pass Josiah and little Peter slivers of dried beef. "And pray, stop that wiggling," he added, since any movements they made dug into the already sore skin on his back.

"Pa! Do ya hear the hounds?" Tom asked in a shaky voice. Si froze and listened.

"Bounty hunters be on the lookout for us!" Charlotte said, in tears again. "They got hounds to catch slaves too!"

"Rest easy, everyone," Si said with a sign of relief. "That is not the sound of yelping dogs. You know we haven't seen a living soul—man, or beast, since leaving the skiff and entering Indiana."

"I'm still scared, Pa," Isaac whined.

"Shhh," Charlotte said, regaining her composure and hugging their second son. "You'll frighten your brothers," but she meant herself as well.

The provisions they'd set out with were running low, and the berries they picked hardly served to satisfy Si and Charlotte, much less their growing boys.

"I'm hungry, Mama." Each child's cry seemed to grab Si's heart like a fist.

One morning Si led his family into a cave, instructing them to wait there until he returned. He was going to fetch them something suitable to eat. Although Si had never begged for food before, he'd spotted several farmhouses near the river and headed towards them now.

"I got nothin' to give any niggers," claimed the woman who opened the door of the first house. "Off with you!"

Si was also ordered away by a man in the second house he knocked at, but as he turned to leave, the man's wife called him back.

"How can you treat any human being so mean?" she

scolded her husband. "We are all God's creatures! Even if a dog were hungry, I would find something for it to eat! Who knows but our own children may someday need the help of a stranger?" Then the woman invited Si inside, motioned him to take a seat at the table, and placed a plate loaded with venison and bread before him. Before he left, she gave him more venison and some cheese and bread. Then, with a smile, she pressed a quarter of a dollar into his hand. Charlotte was so relieved when Si returned safely, bringing food with him, that this time, her tears were tears of joy.

They had nearly reached Cincinnati when Tom sounded another alarm. "Mother's dying," he yelled, causing Si to race back where he found Charlotte lying on the ground. Apparently, she had tripped over a log and fainted. At first Si felt certain he had lost her and became half-mad with fear, since he had no idea how to help her.

"She's coming around," Tom said, and indeed, a few minutes later Charlotte was able to take some fresh spring water and a few mouthfuls of the venison. Following a short rest, Charlotte bravely set out again.

Chapter Thirteen – On The Run

After two weeks of hard travel, the Henson family reached Cincinnati, and Si decided that even if he could get his family no further, they would still be free. Si felt certain that friends he'd made within the black community here would help him find employment, should they decide to remain. There was even more business and bustle in the booming city now than he recalled from his earlier visit.

"Hey there, Henson!" Si's friends welcomed him warmly.

"Good ta see ya again!"

"And this time ya brought yer woman an' young'uns!"

"Come stay with us." A fellow whose name Si had forgotten slapped him on the back. "Plenty of room at my place, and my wife's a fine cook!"

It was sheer delight for their family to find rest and comfort at last. They could finally relax in a galvanized tub and lather off the mud and filth of many weeks. They slept upon soft mattresses, and the Henson boys were given suitable clothing outgrown by friends' children.

"I hear we free in Ohio," Si overheard his son, Tom saying to a companion at dinner.

"Yeah," replied an older man at the table. "But dere're still plenty o' slave-stealers lookin' ta get rich from capturin' black folks."

"Rich an' greedy white masters gotta git their cotton picked," added one freed man. "An' with no more slave ships allowed inta America bringin' negroes from Africa, we all in danger of kidnappin'."

"Gotta keep an eye out all the time for Kentucky spies," their host warned. "Even some free black men be ready an' willin' ta turn in runaways fer de reward."

Charlotte and Si, as well as young Tom, found this table talk quite unsettling. It seemed the free state of Ohio was not the safe place they'd come to believe.

"I think we should press on to Canada like you planned, Papa," Tom said. "I'm scared Kentucky spies will come after us. People are friendly in Cincinnati, but I still don't feel safe here. Why, I've even been told that black children are in the greatest danger of getting kidnapped and sold south."

They had been kindly received in Cincinnati, and for that, Si was most grateful. However, he'd heard some disturbing news that sealed his determination to keep heading north. It seemed that a law had recently been passed in Ohio requiring every black man to post a $500 bond or risk being considered a fugitive slave—and white folks could be fined for harboring a runaway as well as for employing one.

Si was also eager to move on because some Cincinnati friends had told him of a new settlement in Canada that had recently been founded by runaways from this city. It was called Wilberforce in honor of the famous leader of the anti-slavery cause in England. Si decided this place should be their destination.

"Climb in, folks and I'll carry you part-way in my wagon," their host beckoned as they waved goodbyes at the inn and headed for the road. This wagon had a space beneath the floorboards big enough for all four boys to squeeze into and hide.

"You and your wife will be safe riding up here next to me," the driver said. "Long as dere's no broadsides posted about town offerin' rewards for a couple fittin' your description." This friend transported them thirty miles on their way.

"Follow the river," he advised when they climbed out. "An' the North Star. That way, you won't go wrong."

****

"We hungry," Isaac whimpered. The provisions their friends gave them to carry didn't last long traveling with four growing boys. Si's heart wrenched every time one of his children expressed hunger.

Perhaps because they'd been made so comfortable and were so well-treated in Cincinnati, the woods seemed to have become much denser and the nights

77

even darker. They had to wade knee-deep through swamps, and their feet became numb before their trousers and Charlotte's torn pantaloons had any chance to dry. Still, Si dared not light a fire. Tom and Isaac griped incessantly as they wrestled through brambles, fell over exposed roots, and scraped against jagged rocks and bramble bushes.

"We're thirsty."

"Oh, I meant to carry a cup," Si said with sarcasm. "But forgot to pack it."

"But Daddy, I mean we're *really* thirsty." The boys were groaning from eating salted venison.

Josiah considered the matter a moment then headed for the river where he removed both of his shoes. He bent down, filled each shoe to the brim with water and carefully carried them both back to the boys who grinned, giggled, and then drank with delight.

"Lucky my shoes had no holes," he told Charlotte, laughing.

"I trust you rinsed them out well before filling them up with water," she said.

The pain across Si's shoulders and back felt sharper and more constant than before Cincinnati, and Canada seemed even further away than before.

"I don't think I'm going to make it to Canada alive," Charlotte told Si wearily, as they all collapsed in another cave early one morning. "It's too far for me. And this is way too hard. I don't think our boys will last long enough to reach Canada either."

"I know it's a long, hard trek, my dear, but force yourself to keep focused on freedom. We've already made it safely to Northern Ohio."

"These woods are full of wildcats and bears," Charlotte fretted. "I'm afraid Tom will be bitten by a poisonous snake, walking ahead of the rest of us as he insists on doing."

"The only living thing you need to fear, Charlotte," Si said reassuringly, "is man." He didn't let on that he was certain he'd heard wolves howling the previous night and had even made noises to scare them away. Si knew that as long as he lived, 'he would never forget the cries of hunger, thirst, and exhaustion from those he cherished so dearly.'

****

"*Hey*! There's somethin' moving over in those bushes," Tom cried, stopping in his tracks, ever alert for slave-catchers.

Si immediately froze, for he too, had heard the distinct rustling. He realized at once that this particular sound was not caused by some sudden breeze. Could it be a bear with her cubs? He knew mother bears were especially dangerous when they thought their offspring were threatened.

"Just keep going," Josiah told Tom and Charlotte who were both standing still as stone statues.

They continued walking, but the noise followed them. Tom, still in the lead, saw the strangers first. Four Indians not far ahead toted burdens so heavy they were

79

bent down by them. Bows and arrows swung from their bare shoulders. Spotting the Hensons, all four natives immediately vanished into the forest howling.

"Those funny men had hardly anything on!" Isaac said, giggling.

"Most likely they ran home to get the whole tribe to come murder us," Charlotte exclaimed.

"They were carrying bows and arrows," Tom said calmly. "They could have killed us then if they wanted to."

"Oh please, Si, let's turn back," Charlotte pleaded.

"Not a chance," Si told his wife firmly. "There's too much road behind us now. Running from Indians would be ridiculous since they know these woods far better than we do. Anyway, I believe we scared them much more than they frightened us," Si reassured his family. "I'll wager they never saw black folks like us before."

"Will they kidnap us?" asked little Josiah in a soft, scared voice.

"Maybe take us prisoners and torture us?" Isaac wondered.

"Oh, I think not," Si replied confidently. "I've heard tell there are lots of natives around these parts— Shawnee, Chippewa, Ojibwa, Blackhawk, Wyandot tribes, maybe more. I don't believe they're warriors but simple farmers who live in villages."

As the Hensons continued walking, they noticed several natives watching them from behind trees, then dodging out of sight if they caught Si or either of the older boys looking back. Suddenly without warning, the whole family was surrounded by a group of Native Americans, most wearing nothing but loincloths. Their straight black hair hung to their shoulders or was neatly braided.

Some wore colorful headbands with a few feathers struck through. They stared and grinned and chatted among themselves, using words Si had never heard before. They were obviously quite curious as they reached out to touch the boys' tight curls and brown faces. One fellow, apparently the leader, gestured for Si and his family to follow.

"They want us to go along with them," he told Charlotte.

"Where to?" she asked, terrified.

"I have no idea, my dear, but they seem friendly enough."

The Hensons soon found themselves in the midst of a tidy village consisting of wigwams and earthen lodges. Nearby, Si saw healthy crops of what he knew Indians commonly called the Three Sisters –beans, squash, and maize. Melons and pumpkins were abundant, which favorably impressed the farmer in Josiah.

A tall, self-possessed Indian with his arms folded across his bare chest approached. Apparently their chief, he bowed politely, then spoke to his comrades scattered about, perhaps urging them not to be afraid. The Hensons were surrounded by giggling children who touched their arms, pulled at their tattered clothing, and reached out to pat the wooly hair on their heads. Si saw that his own boys were as shy as partridges after spending so much time hiding in the woods. They shrunk away from their Indian counterparts uttering little cries of alarm just as the Shawnee youngsters jumped back as if they feared being bitten.

"Don't worry," Si reassured his sons. "They're simply curious. 'Tis clear they've never before seen people who look as we do."

Si was finally able to convey their destination to the chief and elders, and they were warmly welcomed and presented with a bountiful meal of roast venison and fresh fish, along with harvest vegetables. Si and his family spent a comfortable night inside a wigwam and woke up well rested for the next day's travel. Friends in Cincinnati had advised them to head for a town called Sandusky on Lake Erie, where, if they were lucky, they might catch a boat crossing to Canada.

Several tribesmen accompanied the family a few miles, apparently to make certain they didn't get lost. The Indians pointed out the turn-off towards the lake some twenty-five miles ahead.

Chapter Fourteen – To Buffalo with Captain Burnham

They had their first glimpse of Lake Erie, near Sandusky, also known as Portland. Passing over a portion of Ohio where an extensive plain was found near the lake, they came to a stream. Using a pole, Si forded the water first, then took the three younger boys piggyback across one by one. Even before he carried Charlotte to the other side, he could feel the skin peeling off his back. Yet he sighed with relief when all of them were safe on the other side since the spot they had forded was 100 to 150 yards wide and over four feet deep.

Sandusky was a town of some 500 inhabitants where Si soon noticed a small ship with a gang of men loading cargo. He hid his family in the bushes and told them to await his return. Then he approached the workers.

"Hallo there, man," the captain of the schooner called before Si had even offered himself. "Ya willing to work?"

"Oh yes sir, I sure am," Si shouted back.

"Come along then. I'll give you a shilling for every hour of labor. Got to get this boat loaded if we're gonna get off with this wind." As Si approached the boat, the man looked at him with disappointment, "I'm sorry but you can't work. You're crippled."

"Oh, can't I?" Si said, hoisting a sack of corn behind the line of men who were busy dumping full bags into the hold.

"How far to Canada?" he boldly asked the black man working alongside him, for this fellow somehow seemed to know what was on Si's mind.

"Want to go to Canada, do ye?" he asked as Si nodded in response. "Come along then. Our captain's a fine fellow an' we're soon bound for Buffalo."

"Buffalo?" Si asked. "How far is that from Canada?"

"Why, don't you know, man? Buffalo's just across the river."

"It's not only me, mate," Si said. "My wife and children are with me."

"All right. I'll speak to the captain for you."

A few minutes later, Captain Burnham was standing beside Si. "Hear tell you want to get to Canada?" he asked in a Scotch brogue.

"Yes, sir!" Josiah replied.

"And where's your family now?"

"About a mile back there, Captain, hidin' in some bushes."

"All right then, my fugitive fellow, tell me all about

it. You're running away, are ye not?"

Si immediately sensed this man was a friend, so he opened up with his story.

"I doan like ta see any man gettin' rich on the backs of slaves," Captain Burnham said. "No man has the right to own another, so I'll take my chances an' break the law by transportin' ye. I want to see you get there and be free. I have nothing to give you, for I'm a poor man myself sailin' a boat for wages, but I will see you safe across. Ye won't be the first runaways I've carried across."

Grinning, the captain pointed to the other side of the river. "See those trees over there? Well, those trees are growin' from roots planted in free soil. We're bound for Buffalo, and if the wind stays with us, you'll be there tomorrow evening. Soon as we get this grain loaded, we'll put off from shore, an' I'll send a boat back to pick you up."

Si had never worked with such high spirits as when he joined the other fellows loading grain on this vessel.

The hatches were fastened down, the anchor raised, and sails hoisted when Captain Burnham approached Si to shake his hand. Whispering in his Scotch brogue, he warned, "Do take care, mon. There's lots of kidnappers roamin' these parts huntin' for slaves to catch and sell. They'll surely grab ye if ye bring your family out of hidin' by daylight." Then he promised to send a boat after sundown rather than to take them aboard now at the landing.

Si watched the ship leave her moorings and then

began to fear it might sail without them. For a few terrible moments, Si thought he had been betrayed once again. Then he saw a vessel coming on the wind and lowering a boat for the shore. A few minutes later, his black friend and two sailors jumped onto the beach, and Si soon led them to where he had left Charlotte and the boys in hiding.

"Doan see nobody here," one sailor said as Si's heart lurched.

Where was his family? He was certain this was the exact place he'd left them.

"Charlotte? Tom? Isaac?" Si cried desperately. "Where are you all?"

Paralyzed with fear, he called again. To his great relief, Si then made out their forms in the fading twilight. Charlotte led the boys towards him, then turned and started to run in terror when she saw the other men.

"Stop, Charlotte. It's all right," Si said. "These men are our friends."

"You were gone so long," she said. "I was sure you'd been discovered and carried off." Her eyes were filled with tears as she hugged him. "Oh, Si, I'd given you up for lost—thought I would never more lay eyes on you."

It was but a short row to the boat where, to Si's surprise, he and his family were welcomed aboard with rousing cheers. The crew was as pleased as their captain to assist in the escape.

"All o' ye look plenty tired, an' I kin see that these boys be mighty hungry," one sailor said.

"Well, you're nearly to Canada now! Coom up here on deck an' clap yer wings and craw like a rooster," Captain Burnham said heartily in his thick brogue. "Ye be a free man sure as the devil!"

Si was unable to hold back the tears of joy splashing down his face.

They reached Buffalo the following evening and Black Rock the next morning. The Niagara River was all that separated the slave-holding United States and the Province of Upper Ontario in the free land of Canada.

Captain Burnham saw them onto the ferry to Waterloo. "What will you charge to take this man and his family over?" he asked the ferryman. "He's got no money."

"Three shillings oughta cover it," was the reply, and the captain took a dollar from his pocket and handed it to Si.

"Soon as your feet touch ground agin, you all free," he said, pressing the dollar into Si's hand. Then he placed a big, gentle hand on the top of Si's head. "Be a good fellow now, won't you?" the captain said. "An' use your freedom well."

Si exclaimed, "Yes, I shall use my freedom well!"

"Oh dear, the boys are so filthy," Charlotte fussed as they rode the ferry across. She attempted to pick thorns and briars from her sons' tattered jackets and ripped pants. "Just look at us! We're all covered with caked mud!"

Si saw that Charlotte's skirt and stockings were torn

to shreds. "Dear wife, we are soon free," Josiah said, laughing. "We're sailin' away from danger. Why weep over dirt that's quick to wash away? You're not planning to serve tea to some slaveholder today, are you?"

"Most certainly not," replied Charlotte. "Nor will I ever do so again!"

Chapter Fifteen - The Promised Land

On the morning of October twenty-eight in the year 1830, after six weeks of running, Josiah Henson's feet first touched Canadian soil. He leaped off the ferry before it even docked and threw himself upon the ground. He rolled in the sand and seized handfuls of it. Then he began to dance in circles, cheering like a madman.

"Now, there's one crazy fellow," said a gentleman standing on the levee whom Si would come to know as Colonel Warren. "Perhaps 'tis some unfortunate man felled by a fit."

"Oh no, sir," Si exclaimed, jumping up. "I'm not crazy. Just a free man for the first time!" Si hugged and kissed Charlotte and each one of their sons.

"Oh, is that it?" Colonel Warren asked, laughing at Si's antics. "Never knew freedom to make a man roll in the sand before."

Jubilant that they were no longer another man's

property, Si once again hugged and kissed his wife and boys all round. He had never dared reveal to Charlotte how slim the odds had been against finding 'that haven of promise' called Canada. Yet here 'they were now strangers in a strange land, ragged and penniless.' Si and his family were homeless, hungry, and helpless, but this was the country where they had journeyed to settle. The only thing of importance was that they were no longer six pieces of property belonging to a white master. However, Si knew they must find lodging for tonight, and come tomorrow, he must search for some means of supporting his family.

One fellow at the waterfront informed him that a certain Mister Hibbard might have a job available, so the following morning, Si borrowed a horse and rode out to Hibbard's farm where he was hired on the spot. This prosperous landowner also owned a few small dwellings for workers so the Henson family was provided with a two-story wooden shanty. The place had gone nearly to ruin with the first floor taken over by pigs. Had he risked his own life and the lives of every member of his family to live in a filthy pigpen? Hardly! Si immediately 'expelled the pigs for better types of tenants and went right to work with hoe, shovel, hot water, and a mop.' By midnight, he managed to have the little house in tolerable condition.

Although it was nothing but bare walls when Si brought the rest of the family there the next day, everyone was thrilled with the new home.

"This place is far better than those old slave quarters at Master Riley's place," Charlotte exclaimed with delight.

Si begged straw from Mister Hibbard, and with help from Tom and Isaac, they soon fashioned beds of logs with straw mattresses three feet thick. Hibbard's wife kindly sent over some furniture her family no longer needed.

Then, just as things seemed to finally be going their way, Charlotte and all four boys fell ill—too sick in fact to even rise from their beds or eat. Indeed, Josiah feared he might lose one or even all of them. To come all this way only to have his family die here would be too much to bear. Si was aware that whatever plagued them now was most likely the result of those months of hunger and exhaustion he'd forced them to suffer as fugitives. He nursed each one of them daily with more guilt than the water and gruel he spooned patiently into their mouths. Thankfully, one by one, and to Si's everlasting relief, they all rallied in a few weeks.

The Henson family found food and fuel abundant here, especially after Mister Hibbard gave them a plot of land on which to raise vegetables. Within three years, Si had managed to obtain some pigs, a cow, and a horse he could call his own. Although his new employer was demanding and expected Si to work hard, Hibbard proved quite generous. He was even kind enough 'to cover the cost of Tom's tuition at the nearby school, and the boy soon learned to read fluently and well.'

****

Hearing that the Hensons had arrived in Canada, an old friend of Si's from Maryland, now living in the area, sought him out.

"Are you still preaching these days?" he asked.

"No," replied Si. "I've had no time for that since settling in Canada. Nor have I told anyone in these parts of my ministry."

"Well, you should do so, Henson," his friend urged. "Don't you know you have a gift for preaching?"

This man's encouraging words certainly gave Si something to think about.

****

Tom had become a good reader so Josiah frequently asked his oldest son to read from the Bible, especially on those Sundays he preached. One week, Si rose early and asked Tom to read to him aloud.

"Where shall I read, Father?"

"Oh, anywhere," Si replied, for he had no idea how to direct Tom to any particular verse.

"Who was David, Father?" Tom asked, pausing in his reading.

"A man of God," Si answered, not wishing to admit ignorance to his own child.

"Yes, but I mean exactly *who* was David, Pa? Where was he from? Why is David so important?"

Si realized then that he knew nothing specific about David in the Bible, and he could not lie to his son.

"What's the matter, Father? Can't you read?" Tom

asked Si in amazement. The question was a painful blow to Si's pride. For years, he had pretended to be a literate and learned man.

"No, Tom," he replied, somewhat ashamed. "I never had the opportunity to learn to read. Never had anybody to teach me. You know that in America, it's against the law of the land to teach a slave to read?"

"Well Pa, we're not in America anymore. You can learn to read now."

"Oh no, son, I'm too old to learn. Nor do I have the time for it. I have to work all day so we will have enough to eat."

"Why, that's downright foolish," Tom said. "Nobody's too old to learn to read! You can practice at night."

"But there's no one to teach me. I certainly can't afford to hire a tutor."

"Then I shall teach you, Father," exclaimed Tom. "I can do it, and you will be able to talk better and preach better once you can read!"

So Si swallowed his pride and agreed to try. Soon he and Tom were sharing lessons by the light of some hickory bark or pine-knot every evening.

Progress proved painfully slow, and both Si and his son often grew discouraged. Tom frequently lost patience with his father's little scratches on the slate and sighed over Si's ignorance like a stern schoolmaster addressing a stupid boy. Tom sometimes even fell asleep during sessions.

Struggling over the *Primer*, Si felt his bitterness towards slavery renewed along with the oppression beneath which he had been forced to live and toil so long. He knew slaveholders purposely kept their slaves in an abyss of ignorance in order to control investments in their property. It made Si more determined than ever to do something for the rescue and elevation of blacks suffering the evils he had endured. Most of these poor people did not even realize how degraded and ignorant they were, thought Si.

****

Josiah and his family learned that Canada was a cold place with long, frigid winters, yet blacks living in Canada were granted citizenship and full rights along with all other immigrants. No one stood around ordering you to do something to please them. Here, men and women could decide things for themselves and were permitted to live where they pleased. They could earn real money from the jobs they performed, and here, in Canada, a black man could start up his own business and buy land to farm if he so desired. Black citizens in Canada even had the right to vote and could serve on juries.

Si found himself reflecting more and more on the circumstances of black immigrants whose numbers continued to increase almost daily. Runaway refugees from the states crossed into Canada, yet after experiencing initial joy at their safe deliverance, they saw little improvement in their daily lives.

Although many arrived with a basic understanding of agricultural methods, these former slaves seldom enjoyed prosperity in their new environment. Indeed, many seemed to lack ambition and were content with earning a day's pay for a day's work. Simply happy to finally be free, most were generally satisfied to put themselves out for hire to work lands belonging to others rather than aspiring to become independent proprietors. Si wanted to awaken these former slaves to the advantages that now lay within their reach.

Josiah Henson worked for Hibbard three years and then accepted a position with Benjamin Riseley, an employer with a wider vision for the future of Canada's former slave population. Riseley seemed eager to cooperate with Si in an attempt to awaken the immigrants to new opportunities. He hosted meetings in his home to discuss possibilities. The dozen who regularly assembled there finally agreed to pool some portion of their earnings in order to obtain land they could call their own—where every tree felled and every bushel of corn raised would be for themselves—a place to call their own, where they might become self-sufficient and enjoy the profits of their labor. Energy, enterprise, and self-reliance would guide this vision and venture.

Encouraged by his associates, Si journeyed more than 300 miles into the wilderness over the next two years, chiefly by foot, scouting for the ideal site to establish a community where former slaves might become their own masters. At this time, the Canadian government was opening tracts for settlement from Lake Erie to the Detroit River. Si traveled an extensive region between the lakes of Ontario, Erie, and Huron until he finally arrived east of Lake St. Clair and the Detroit River.

He was greatly impressed by the fertility of the soil there and promptly recommended the place to his associates. Wisely cautious however, they sent Si off again so he might observe this area during different seasons. It still looked good to Si, yet after traveling a little further, he discovered an extensive tract of government land near Colchester that had been granted to a Mr. McCormick who was eager to rent it out. This land had already been cleared for planting, so Si decided they should first settle there, and then, with further proceeds acquired, purchase the place he would call *Dawn*, to mark the new day.

As it turned out, McCormick had neglected to comply with the conditions of his land grant and thus was not entitled to rent. On the advice of Sir John Cockburn, Si and his associates took the case to the legislature. After a second appeal, they were freed from all rent payments as long as they remained. Though the new settlers farmed this property some seven years, it was still not their own land, which meant the Canadian government could sell it out from under them at any time.

****

In 1836, Si became acquainted with Hiram Wilson, now a missionary in Cholchester. In 1835, Wilson had left Oberlin College in Ohio for Upper Canada on behalf of the American Anti-Slavery Society, to see how fugitives were faring. He established several schools in the growing black communities. Wilson claimed there was a shortage of clergymen in Canada and encouraged Si to actively pursue a career in the ministry here.

The two men commenced preaching together at outdoor camp meetings, and Si soon realized that people were willing to travel long distances to hear him preach. Henson's sermons did not only focus on Biblical texts but offered his congregations practical knowledge for daily life.

'I insisted on the necessity of raising one's own crops, and saving their wages, thus reaping the profits of their own labor,' Henson later wrote. He and Hiram Wilson both believed it was only through education and self-sufficiency that free blacks would truly become free.

Si inspired audiences to strive to better themselves through education and even offered practical advice on farming methods from the pulpit. He encouraged the fugitives' independence, warning them to no longer be so willing to work for some other man's benefit but to set goals of buying their own land. Si also preached against the evils of slavery—how Africans had been kidnapped from their homelands, locked in chains, and forced into backbreaking labor in order to make white men wealthy. These immigrants had been raised in ignorance and dependence and desperately needed guidance. They faced poverty when they arrived in Canada, unaccustomed to making decisions or managing their own destiny.

Hiram Wilson proved as enthusiastic as Si about establishing a permanent settlement for ex-slaves in Canada. Wilson contacted James Canning Fuller, his wealthy Quaker friend and a philanthropist from England then living in New York State, who promptly sent them fifteen hundred dollars donated by English Quakers. In June of 1838, Henson and Wilson held a convention in London, Upper Canada, inviting black residents from surrounding areas to join them in deciding how best to spend the donation. It was finally agreed upon to use the money to establish a manual-labor school where children of fugitive slaves could be taught not only traditional grammar school subjects but also mechanic arts, with domestic arts offered the girls. Originally known as the British-American Institute, it was a school for Education of Mental, Moral, & Physical of the Coloured Inhabitants of Canada, not excluding White Persons and Indians.

Chapter Sixteen - *Dawn* of a New Day

"You're just the man to do it," Hiram Wilson told Josiah. "You are a natural leader, Henson—knowledgeable and practical enough to make an enterprise such as this meet with success."

In June of 1838, Josiah Henson purchased 200 acres of rich, uncultivated land at $4 an acre. Thickly forested with black walnut, white oak, ash, hickory, and maple trees, it was situated at the bend of Sydenham River in Chatham, Ontario, near the township of Dresden, a hundred miles east of Detroit, Michigan. The Hensons were living here by 1842. Then with financial assistance, Si purchased another 200 adjoining acres to establish *Dawn Institute* where former slaves could learn the practical skills that would enable them to become self-sufficient. The land was cleared for tillage and soon, former slaves began relocating here with their own families. Henson then sold a hundred acres of his own land to the Institute at a discounted rate and the new educational enterprise soon comprised a total of 300 acres.

The American Manual Labor Institute, soon renamed the British -American Institute, opened in December, 1842 with twelve boarding students housed in a large log cabin. Hiram Wilson taught academics and 'expounded spiritual truths' at the new grammar school where black and Indian children could be educated without harassment by white children or discrimination by adults—a place where all children were treated as equals. Enrollment quickly grew so that additional teachers were recruited from Oberlin College in Ohio.

Students spent half of each day in the classroom and the remainder, cutting timber or working the farm. At this training school, boys could learn agriculture, blacksmithing, rope-making, brick manufacture, as well as milling and carpentry skills that would enable them to become economically independent. Girls were instructed in 'those domestic arts that are the proper occupation and ornament of their sex.' Within a decade, 116 students were in attendance.

Livestock abounded at Dawn, and fences stood in good order. The community had no tavern or grog shop, but a chapel was located near the schoolhouse. Although Henson's dream of a self-sufficient community of free blacks was proving a viable enterprise, the financial struggle to maintain it remained constant. Farming, by its very nature, was always risky, and even more so in this cold, uncertain climate. However, Henson could boast of the industry of these former slaves who, when in bondage, could not claim ownership of anything, not even their own children. At Dawn, they got right to work clearing gardens and small farms, hiring themselves out as woodsmen to earn money cutting timber until each man was able to purchase or lease his own land.

Huge black walnut trees abounded on the property, and as these were felled to clear the land for planting, Si and his associates decided to open a sawmill to process lumber. The Sydenham River was navigable so lumber could be easily shipped to Detroit, and from there, to other parts of the United States or across the Atlantic to England.

Substantial funding would be required for this venture, so Si traveled through New England visiting sawmills and observing various lumber enterprises. Wherever Henson journeyed, he spread news and sang praises about Dawn, resulting in generous donations from abolitionists and other interested parties. And always, he lectured on the evils of slavery.

"I wish I had entire control of southern slaveholders for twenty-four hours," he told an audience in Boston's Tremont Temple. A man seated in the front row immediately stood up.

"May I ask the speaker one question?" he asked.

"Mr. Henson has the platform. No one is permitted to interrupt him without his permission," cautioned the moderator.

"Allow the fellow to speak," Si urged.

"And pray, Mr. Henson, what would you do with those southern slaveholders?"

"Well, first I would have them all converted to God, and secondly, I would send them immediately to heaven before they had one minute to backslide," Si informed the audience, resulting in an uproar of cheers.

Si raised one thousand dollars in Boston to build the sawmill at Dawn. He also managed to develop new markets for the Canadian community's lumber business.

"'Tis high time you told your story in print, Josiah," Hiram Wilson and others urged Si. "You spent what, some thirty years as a plantation slave, then ran away to start a colony for your fellow fugitives here in Canada. Most folks would enjoy reading about that! You know slave narratives are all the rage in the northern states these days. Your tale could bring in some real cash for the British-American Institute at Dawn, not to mention the entire anti-slavery movement."

So Josiah Henson told his story to the former mayor of Boston and renowned abolitionist, Samuel Aikens Eliot, who meticulously copied down the events and details of his life in bondage as Si dictated them.

"You have the natural eloquence of a writer," Eliot told Si. "Indeed, it is the same gift you express whenever you preach." With his son Tom's help, Si reread Eliot's pages numerous times, painstakingly making changes, cuts, and additions he felt important to make throughout. *The Life of Josiah Henson: Formerly a Slave; Now an Inhabitant of Canada, Narrated by Himself* was published in Boston by Arthur D. Phelps in 1849 and was an immediate success.

Chapter Seventeen - The Crystal Palace

The beautifully polished black walnut boards of finest grain and texture fashioned at Dawn's lumber mill were suitable for ornamental use, so in 1851, Si decided to show some examples at the Crystal Palace in Hyde Park, London. This exposition, the first of its kind, was the talk of the civilized world, featuring the latest inventions and products from all over the world, including Great Britain's Colonies of Australia, New Zealand, India, and Canada. If art and industry was the theme, then Si would select some of Dawn's prize examples and travel to London and put them on exhibit.

Amos A. Lawrence of Boston, the anti-slavery enthusiast who amassed a fortune from textile mills in the new Massachusetts cities of Lowell and Lawrence, helped finance Henson's trip to England.

Si oversaw the stacked black walnut boards as they were loaded onto an American vessel. They were excellent specimens, about seven foot in length and four feet in width, of superb grain and texture. Upon arrival in England, he had them planed and polished so they shone like mirrors.

Si soon received complaints from American participants regarding his entry of Canadian products for exhibition having been shipped across the Atlantic on a vessel belonging to the United States, so he hired a painter to print a sign in large white letters to hang over his booth.

This is the product of the industry of a fugitive slave from the United States whose residence is Dawn, Canada.

Henson joined 15,000 fellow exhibitors showcasing recent technology. There were more than ten miles of display area beneath the famous glass dome. An estimated six million people attended this first world's fair to view the many new inventions and amazing wonders from around the globe.

'Perhaps it was my complexion that attracted attention since I was the only black person with a booth, but nearly all who passed paused to look at me and at themselves, reflected in my black walnut mirrors.'

One of the many admirers of Josiah Henson's products was Queen Victoria herself who attended the Crystal Palace with her cortege. Josiah overheard Her Majesty ask a companion, "Is he truly a fugitive slave?"

"He is indeed, your majesty, and that is his work,"

was the reply.

Si was awarded a bronze medal for the 'quality of craftsmanship' of his decorative walnut cabinets. He was also presented with a portrait of the British Royal Family.

Queen Victoria had a keen interest in the increasing discord and national hostility over the issue of slavery in the United States. Josiah knew the queen to be an enemy of slavery even though her nation was economically dependent upon cotton imported from the American South. When the Fugitive Slave Law went into effect in the United States in 1850, Queen Victoria announced, 'As slavery cannot exist on British soil, no runaway who reaches Canada will ever be returned south.'

Si remained in England after the Crystal Palace closed to speak in British churches concerning the plight of slaves in the United States. He addressed attentive audiences some ninety-nine times in churches, schools, and other public venues during this sojourn in England. He also visited the King Edward Industrial School as well as a school for girls in Scotland.

He managed to raise a thousand English pounds for Dawn's school and community needs, including a hefty sum donated by the Foreign Anti-Slavery Society. He left these funds with Samuel Gurney, a London treasurer who had helped secure the emancipation of slaves in the West Indies.

Mister Gurney publicly claimed that 'Dawn could be made the brightest spot in the garden of the Lord if there were only an efficient manager at the head to control it.' Gurney vowed to clear the entire enterprise out of debt and turn it into 'a moral lighthouse whose beacon would be permanent.'

It was Samuel_Gurney who introduced Si to the archbishop of Canterbury.

"At what university did you graduate, sir?" the Archbishop asked Si after they had been properly introduced.

"I graduated, your grace, from the *School of Adversity*," Josiah promptly replied. "It was my lot to be born a slave and to pass my first forty years in bondage. I never went to school but received my training under the most adverse circumstances."

"Why, Mr. Henson, I never suspected you to be anything less than a formally educated man."

Lord Henry George Grey, the Queen's home secretary, later approached Henson with the suggestion he travel to India to supervise that British colony's cotton interests. Although Si found this quite flattering and definitely a tempting offer, he knew his true interests and commitments were with *Dawn*.

"I know nothing of growing cotton, my lord," Josiah told the nobleman. "Cotton did not grow on the farms I formerly supervised in Maryland and Kentucky."

In June of 1852, Lord John Russell, England's Prime Minister, invited Si to dine at his residence, a palatial estate set amid beautiful gardens filled with an amazing variety of songbirds. Josiah was seated at the head of the table in the spacious dining room with some 300 guests. He was asked to say the blessing and he sang for them:

Be present at our table, Lord
Be here and everywhere adored. These
creatures bless
And grant that we may feast In Paradise with
Thee.

After dinner, when called upon to offer a toast, Josiah raised his glass and declared, 'First to England, honor to the brave, freedom to the slave, success to British emancipation. God bless the Queen!'

"Up! Up, again!" came the cheers from the crowd seated around the tables.

So Si stood once more to hail Her Majesty. 'To our most sovereign lady, the Queen. May she have a long life, and an easy death. May she reign in righteousness and rule in love. And to her illustrious Consort, Prince Albert, may he have peace at home, pleasure abroad, love his Queen, and serve the Lord.'

Henson was still in England, lecturing and fundraising when on the third of September 1852, he received word that Charlotte was gravely ill. Two days later, he boarded the *Canada*, the first steamship departing Liverpool, and was bound for Boston. Four of his daughters, amazed to find their father back home in Dawn, rushed out the front door to greet him. Si spent the next few weeks at Charlotte's bedside.

My beloved wife, companion of my life, sharer of my

joys and sorrows. Charlotte had been unwell for a number of years; still, when she died in 1852, it was a heartbreaking loss for Si and their children.

Dear Charlotte had demonstrated great courage remaining by his side throughout those uncertain years of slavery; then traveling with him, fearful and footsore, across the perilous wilderness out of the land of bondage to safe refuge in Canada.

'We had a few weeks left together before she sank into quiet sleep,' Si would later recall. 'We talked over our whole past life together, reviewing scenes of sorrow and trouble, as well as our many bright and happy days spent together.'

Charlotte's death left Si desolate and painfully lonesome. His beloved companion and affectionate friend of forty years was gone, and Si's heart and home seemed unbearably empty.

****

Soon after returning home, Henson discovered that Peter Smith, the Dawn resident he left in charge of the lumber mill when he sailed to England, had disappeared. After ordering three ships loaded with lumber but without paying some forty workers the wages they had earned, the fellow simply vanished. These employees were understandably incensed, and in frustration and fury, they destroyed the lumber mill.

'When that saw mill was gone, I felt as if I'd lost an old friend,' Si later wrote. The worst of it was that they would not be able to fill the orders for lumber that he had recently negotiated in England.

John Scoble turned out to be another major disappointment even though the British anti-slavery leader had raised a thousand pounds for the Dawn community. Appointed resident superintendent, Scoble had taken possession of the entire farm belonging to the Dawn Institute and proceeded to purchase expensive farm machinery and prize cattle, plunging the farm into serious debt.

Also, Dawn's original school building had become too run down for use, but Scoble's promises for new buildings and improvements on the old ones never materialized.

Si finally confronted him. "The people are growling," he told John Scoble. "When will you start the new school building?"

"Let them growl," Scoble replied. "I did not come here to have coloured people dictate to me!"

"If you do not intend to build, you'd best leave the farm and let us manage for ourselves," Josiah told the pompous Englishman.

"Then pay me what I have expended these past years, and I will go," demanded Scoble. "I have tried my best to make this place meet expenses."

Si realized he had been deceived by yet another white man. He had trusted John Scoble too easily, just as he had both Riley brothers. However, this time, he was a free man so he could summon the law and take John Scoble to court. Over the next seven years, a series of costly lawsuits and counter lawsuits ensued, which eventually forced Henson to mortgage Dawn farm.

However, by 1852, Dawn had a population of 500 free black families situated on 1500 acres near Dresden with some sixty students attending the school. Henson estimated another thirty-five hundred former fugitives, and their families lived within a day's journey from Dawn.

'With but a few exceptions,' Josiah claimed, 'all were refugees from slavery. This settlement is a perfect success,' Si liked to remind all who visited. 'Here are men bred in slavery who came here and purchased land at government prices, cleared it, bought their own implements, built their own houses and now, support themselves.'

****

In 1858, Josiah married the widow, Nancy Oakes whom he first met on a fund-raising trip to Boston. Nancy was a Sunday school teacher and active in church affairs. Raised in a Quaker household in Baltimore, she had received a good education. Nancy's parents had been slaves, but her mother earned enough money as a laundress to buy her freedom as well as that of Nancy's father. Several more trips to Boston were required before Si summoned the courage to ask Nancy to marry him.

Henry Bleby, a Boston acquaintance and biographer of Henson described him at this time as 'blithe and active as a youth of sixteen.' Bleby offered the following word picture: 'The Reverend Henson was of middle size, firm and well knit, clothed in a new glossy suit of clerical broadcloth… all over black, except for his sparkling cravat and a set of pearly white teeth. Again and again did laughter spread over his countenance and tell of a rollicking, fun-loving spirit that could not often be clouded with gloom. On looking more closely as he stood before me, holding a glossy white beaver hat in one hand while he extended the other in friendly salutation, I observed that both his arms were crippled so that he could by no means use them freely... with rollicking enjoyment he related the experiences of his Canadian life, always looking on the bright side.'

It was on one of these fund-raising trips to Boston that Si apparently met Harriet Beecher Stowe. According to Charles and Lyman Stowe, the famous author's son and grandson, the two met in Boston in January of 1850 at the home of her brother, the Reverend Edward Beecher. Active in the anti-slavery cause, Beecher and his family had recently returned to Boston from Illinois. He was editor of *The Congregationist* and a former pastor of Park Street Church (*McClures' Magazine*, 36 (1911), p. 613-4).

Mrs. Stowe was eager to learn more about slavery, and it may have been Josiah Henson who told her about the real—life 'Eliza,' whom he met in Canada. Si heard the young woman describe her daring escape on ice floes across the Ohio River, carrying her baby in her arms. Having buried a child of her own not long before, Stowe was particularly horrified at the thought of slave mothers sold away from their children.

Since passage of the revised Fugitive Slave Act by U. S. Congress in 1850, Boston had become a hotbed of abolitionism. The North was now filled with slave-hunters on horseback, often accompanied by trained dogs. Ready to administer quick and cruel punishment, they carried whips and guns and could legally stop any black person to demand a pass or manumission papers. It was not unusual to see a band of these bounty hunters pulling captured slaves behind their horses with ropes around their necks.

Now any black person, including freed slaves, could be apprehended as property in any place and sent back to their previous owners. Any slave caught off his master's place was liable to be seized and whipped by any white man. Even blacks born free were now in peril of being kidnapped and sold into slavery or sent back to any white man who claimed ownership. And any white person guilty of assisting a suspected runaway was liable to imprisonment and a heavy fine.

No person, black or white, could be trusted. With rewards offered for information on runaways, even former slaves were often more than willing to turn over fugitives for any promise of privileges or reward money. Every black man, woman, or child lived in fear of betrayal and seizure.

It was this cruel law that inspired Harriet Beecher Stowe to write *Uncle Tom's Cabin or Life Among the Lowly,* first published in serial form in the anti-slavery journal *National Era*. Her book released in 1852, was an overnight sensation and international bestseller with more than a million copies sold in England in one year, along with some 300,000 in the United States.

****

"There's a fellow been asking for you," a friend who resided in Dawn told Josiah one day. "Says he's some sort of agent on the underground railway. His name is William Champlain, and it seems he's got some personal news for you."

"I believe that your brother, Jacob Henson, was one of my passengers on the underground railroad," Champlain told Si. "You see, I was bringing this fellow Henson and some other slaves off a Georgia plantation, but we got caught. I'd still be rotting in prison if those good Quaker folks hadn't bailed me out."

"Jacob? My brother Jacob!" exclaimed Josiah, dumbfounded. He had forced himself years ago to cease thinking about his brothers and sisters. Si assumed that if they were not all dead by now, they were surely lost to him forever.

"Where is Jacob now?" Si finally managed to ask. "Did he go to prison with you?"

"Oh no. He got sold off and sent to a tobacco plantation in Maryland."

"Then I must find a way to bring him here," exclaimed Si. "Jacob deserves to be free like me."

Si was eventually able to learn that Jacob's master would agree to sell his brother for the sum of $550.

Determined to raise enough money to buy his brother out of bondage, Si published an expanded version of his 1849 slave narrative giving it the new, more dramatic title of *Truth Stranger than Fiction: Father Henson's Story of His Own Life*. For this version, he added sections about his trip to England and lecture tours there. Amos Lawrence, who had financed Si's previous trip to England, agreed to pay for this new publication with assistance from other Boston-area abolitionists. Mister Lawrence also suggested Si request a recommendation for this book from Harriet Beecher Stowe.

Even though, as a fugitive slave, Si was in danger of being captured and sold south, he traveled by train to Andover, where the author lived with her husband, Calvin Stowe, a professor at Andover Theological Seminary, and their children. Si intended to ask Mrs. Stowe to write a *puff-piece* recommending his revised and expanded autobiography to potential readers.

Many readers believed that Mrs. Stowe adapted Uncle Tom's rescue of little Eva from hearing how Henson had saved Susan St. Clair Young from her own watery death. Susan was the daughter of Isaac Riley's Kentucky neighbor, a farmer who freed all his slaves. The Stowes graciously received Josiah, and what she wrote pleased him immensely:

> *The numerous friends of the author of this little work will need no greater recommendation than his name to make it welcome. Among all*

the interesting records to which the institution of American slavery has given rise, we know of none more characteristic than that of Josiah Henson. Our excellent friend has prepared this edition of his work for the purpose of redeeming from slavery a beloved brother.

The book was published in Boston by John P. Jewett and Company in 1858 and released in London the following year.

Josiah then took to the road, traveling all over New England, his saddlebags loaded with copies to sell. A bank in Boston sympathetic to the anti-slavery cause added to what Si earned from book sales and quickly dispatched $550 to Baltimore contacts who obtained manumission papers for Si's brother and arranged his passage on a ship sailing to Boston. By the time Si returned to Dawn, he had more than enough money to transport Jacob to Canada.

Still, Si realized he'd spent too much time away from Dawn. He returned to find that the Court of Chancery had appointed a new board of trustees for the Institute. They had decided to sell land belonging to the school and after paying debts owed, to establish a new school at Chatham called The Wilberforce Educational Institute in honor of the English anti-slavery parliamentarian.

Josiah was anxiously waiting on the wharf when the vessel delivering his long lost brother docked. Although they remembered each other slightly as small boys, it might as well have been their initial meeting. Josiah and Jacob ran sobbing into each other's outstretched arms, and words tumbled from the two of them at once. As they stood there hugging, both became keenly aware of the family resemblance and spoke tearfully of their mother and lost brothers and sisters.

Chapter Eighteen - Slave-Stealer

Soon after Si's brother joined the Dawn community, James Lightfoot traveled from Fort Erie in Ontario, seeking Henson on behalf of his enslaved family. Lightfoot's parents, three sisters, and four brothers remained in bondage near Maysville, Kentucky.

"Last I heard, all of my folks livin' on Frank Taylor's plantation on the Ohio River. Can you bring 'em out?" he pleaded. "Won't you find some way to shepherd them safely here?"

It was the first time Si had considered venturing back into the United States with the precarious purpose of guiding fugitive slaves to Canada on the underground railroad. He knew that going back could mean capture, torture or prison, even worse, spending the rest of his life in slavery—an unbearable thought after having lived a free man for years. Did he dare chance losing his own liberty and his new life in Canada?

"My old master thinks me dead," Lightfoot

explained. "If I went back to fetch my family, I'd be killed on the spot for sure."

After Si tasted freedom himself, his mind often dwelt on those who still suffered captivity, and he came to realize that he must find some way to free as many slaves as he possibly could. Because of his own family's flight, Si knew he was in a position to offer others sound advice on how to escape.

Yet serving as a shepherd to escort runaway slaves to freedom was something Si considered long and carefully before he agreed to travel the perilous journey back across the border and south into Kentucky. Lightfoot was hardly alone in hoping to rescue other family members, for it seemed that whenever new fugitives set foot in Canada, they fixed their minds on rescuing loved ones left behind. They would search desperately for familiar faces in hopes of a reunion on Canadian soil with family members sold away from their sides long ago. Josiah had witnessed several such reunions and was deeply moved by their joy after decades of separation. The many former slaves Josiah had come to know in Canada made him more determined than ever to do something for the rescue and elevation of those suffering the same evils that he and his family had once endured. His anger was riled whenever he thought of all that slavery had deprived him of in life.

Si knew it was incredibly dangerous to serve as a shepherd on the underground railroad, yet how could he not attempt to conduct others to the same freedom he now enjoyed? No one should be forced to suffer the horrendous evils of slavery. Every man, woman, and child should have the chance to strike out for liberty. They all deserved the opportunity to make a new life in a free society and find the safe haven he and his family had found. Si` vowed to serve as a modern Moses and lead others to the Promised Land.

'I was glad to help such of my old friends as had the spirit to make the attempt to free themselves. I might enable others to follow in my footsteps for I knew the routes pretty well and had much greater facilities for traveling now than when I came out of that Egypt with my family the first time.'

Since the passage of the Fugitive Slave Act in 1850, no black felt safe in America, and more and more fugitives headed for the Canadian border. By 1860, 500 fugitives were arriving every year. And slaveholders hired an increasing number of slave hunters to recapture their legal property from bold slave-stealers like Josiah Henson.

"I will return to Kentucky, Lightfoot, and do my best to lead your family into Canada," Si finally agreed.

"Take this with you," James Lightfoot said, handing Si a polished stone. "Any member of my family will recognize it and know to put their trust in following you."

When Si finally managed to locate the Lightfoot family, he found James' parents too old to venture any trip, while James' sisters were married and had too many children to consider leaving Maysville. His four brothers were able to travel but thought it would be too painful to leave the rest of the family behind. They also feared Taylor's other slaves might reveal any attempt they made to escape, so in the end, they declined to accompany Si.

"Will you come back a year from now?" they asked. "And show us the way to Canada then?" Si agreed to return, and then made his way into the interior of Kentucky, having heard that a group of thirty slaves was waiting there for a leader.

Si did return to rescue the Lightfoot family a year later as promised, though it turned out to be a narrow escape. At one point, on his way back to Maysville, 'to avoid being questioned by authorities, I stuffed dry leaves into a scarf and bound it around my face up to my eyes, pretending to be unable to speak and affected in both brain and body. Waiting for the boat that evening, I was asked to whom I belonged but merely shook my head, mumbling incoherently so they left me alone.' Upon landing, Si met James Lightfoot's brother, Jefferson, and together, they seized a skiff to make their way down river, but the boat sprang a leak, and they both nearly drowned.

The two men then joined the rest of the Lightfoots but missed the stage at Cincinnati. The Miami River had to be crossed in order to reach the city, and they walked up and down the riverbank, trying to find a place to cross as the group grew increasingly anxious. Si decided to humor them.

"Let us try again up river," he said cheerfully, 'for I saw a cow coming out of the woods there. Let's go see that cow, for she may tell us what we need to know'

"That cow cannot talk," Jefferson Lightfoot said.

But at that moment, the cow walked right through the river as if telling them the exact place to cross. It had started to snow when the youngest Lightfoot lad had a seizure and had to be carried. They hiked through snow, mud, and rain, finally reaching Cincinnati on a Sunday morning where they hid out until Monday evening.

Some distance down the road, they saw a white man approaching by foot but were not alarmed after he told them he had been living in the south and was now fleeing his employers. He joined the group and saved them from slave hunters who were close on their tracks. Having walked all night, they stopped at an inn where their white companion ordered breakfast for six.

Si instinctively sensed danger and urged the group to immediately follow him outside, which they were reluctant to do at first, not wishing to forfeit the meal. However, they all went into the yard and began walking although the snow was up to their knees. Suddenly they heard the tramping of horses and quickly dove behind bushes. The slave-hunters halted their horses in front of the inn. Therefore, Si knew had they remained inside, they would have been apprehended. Their white friend was questioned at the door. Had he seen any blacks passing by?

"Yes, sir."

"Oh? How many?"

"About six, I think".

"Which way did they go?"

"In the direction of Detroit, I believe."

The slave hunters reined their horses and soon rode off, so Si and the Lightfoots ventured inside to finish breakfast. The innkeeper even offered to sail the group in his boat across to Canada.

Then the youngest Lightfoot became so sick it seemed doubtful he would survive. They made a litter from their shirts to carry the boy and traveled by day keeping to the woods. The boy grew no better and begged to be left behind so the entire company would not be captured. With great reluctance, they laid him in a sheltered spot, expecting death to soon end his suffering.

The group had trudged a few miles when one of the boy's brothers stopped, explaining he was unable to go on knowing he'd left his little brother to perish alone. His grief was so great that they all decided to go back where they discovered the poor boy moaning with every breath he took.

Just then, a wagon approached.

"Where is thee headed?" inquired the carter.

The words 'Thee' and 'thou' indicated Quaker faith, so Si replied, "To Canada, sir."

The man reined in his horses and offered assistance. When he noticed the sick boy, he turned his horses back toward his house instead of proceeding on his way to market. Si and the Lightfoots spent the night with the Quaker and his wife, and then left the boy behind in their care as the rest of the group pushed on to Lake Erie.

Leading other fugitives a few months later, Si returned to the home of the Quaker couple and found the young boy in robust health. He was soon reunited with the rest of the Lightfoots in Canada.

Not long after this, Frank Taylor, the owner of this large family of slaves, fell ill and 'was persuaded by friends to free the rest of the Lightfoots, which he did, making it possible for them all to be reunited in the Promised Land.'

The precarious trip to lead the Lightfoots out of bondage was but one of many missions Henson made south to steal slaves in the years that followed. Si believed every human being had the right to his or her own body, so he eventually traveled by foot through New York State, Pennsylvania, Ohio, Kentucky, and even back into Maryland. Sometimes, more than thirty runaways from various states would gather in a designated place, eagerly awaiting to follow Josiah Henson across the Ohio River. He often led fugitives through Richmond, Indiana, a town founded by Quakers, where the runaways were treated to kindness and rest and nourishment before continuing on their way through the wilderness to Toledo on the western shore of Lake Erie, eventually finding passage by fishing boat or trade vessel into Canada.

Before they set out on the trip north, Si cautioned his followers that the road to freedom would be a treacherous one. "Take no one into your confidence," he would warn them. And since he knew the various routes increasingly well, each trip became easier, though he expected he would never grow accustomed to climbing over felled trees or wrestling his way through brambles that bloodied one's face. He soon learned which houses welcomed runaways—who was a friend to be trusted to answer their knock on the door and offer food and shelter; a safe house where the group might hide and sleep another day in some crawl space or hidey-hole before fleeing once more after dark. Si also came to know the best hiding places in the forest and which men drove wagons with false floors that allowed runaways to crouch beneath.

"We travel light," Si informed all runaways. "Swear to secrecy and trust no one. Do not dare look to another person for help." Nor would Si listen when one of his charges begged him to turn back because they felt certain they'd heard hounds or the hoof beats of some bounty hunter on their trail.

"You will gain your freedom or be ready to die in the attempt," Si warned, for he knew *Wanted* signs would sure to be posted advertising their escapes and that dogs would most likely be set on hunting them down. Kidnappers, greedy to earn bounties and toting whips and firearms, were ever on the lookout.

"Keep an open eye, for the closer we get to the

Canadian border, the more slave catchers will be around, eager to capture you and sell you off. You will suffer hunger," Si informed his charges truthfully, although he always distributed victuals for them to carry on the road: strips of smoked venison, salt herring, dried fruit, cornbread, cheese, and the like. "Should the worse come, we can always survive on nuts and berries gathered along the way."

Si told them that the hard trip ahead would not only require physical energy and endurance, but that which was most necessary —hope. Si often kept spirits up by singing. *Follow the Drinking Gourd seemed* to be everyone's favorite.

> *I'll meet you in the morning*
> *When I reach the Promised Land*
> *On the other side of Jordan.*
> *For I'm bound for the Promised Land.*

Si lost count of the number of trips he made back and forth delivering fugitives across the Canadian border, not to mention how many times he crossed the Ohio River. There were some incredibly difficult sojourns through winter gales when his little band, close to freezing, journeyed across Lake Erie upon ice.

Other seasons, he told his followers to wrap their feet in rags to make it easier to run through woods without suffering scratches and cuts, something he wished he'd known to advise his family on their own escape to Canada.

Though in constant danger of recapture, Henson remained deeply committed to liberating slaves. He enjoyed referring to himself as 'a devotee of abduction.' Asked to later recall those rescue missions, Si estimated he'd delivered some 118 individuals out of enslavement.

When a southern sympathizer he once met in Cincinnati demanded 'to know how Si dared to shamelessly steal another man's property, Henson replied, 'The shame is not on me but upon the slave holders. We are but following the light of liberty.'

When Si's passengers finally arrived in Canada as free men and women, they inevitably wept for joy, kissed the earth, and often danced along the shore just as Si himself had once done.

In Canada, the Land of Liberty, one could enjoy the fruits of one's own labor and any_former slave could earn his own livelihood by asserting himself. After a few years, with honest and hard work, immigrants could own their own farms, raise all sorts of grains and vegetables, and cultivate a variety of fruit trees. They could sit under their own vine and fig trees. Henson always told his new arrivals in Canada that 'liberty was a glorious hope not as an escape from toil but as an avenue to self-respect and some ennobling occupation.'

"Do you not find the cold Canadian winters long and unpleasant?" folks often asked Si.

To this question, he always replied, 'Cool freedom is far better than hot oppression.'

Chapter Nineteen - To See The Queen Again

In 1876, Josiah Henson sailed to England and Scotland again, this time accompanied by his wife, Nancy. He was determined to raise enough money to clear the heavy mortgage on the farm that he had been forced to levy to meet the cost of the long lawsuit over the Dawn Institute property. Josiah had to bear the entire expense of that lawsuit himself.

They had been invited for an audience with Queen Victoria, so on the fifth of March, they traveled by train to Windsor Castle. John Lobb, managing editor of *Christian Age Magazine*, accompanied them on the royal visit along with a popular spiritualist who was then leading séances throughout England. Lobb edited the 1876 version of Si's *Narrative* and even published a book for young people on Henson's life.

The visitors, all formally attired, were treated to luncheon at 1:00, and at 3:00 o'clock, the Queen made her appearance with Prince Leopold and Princess Beatrice, accompanied by lords and ladies-in-waiting. Her Majesty also invited her staff to meet 'Uncle Tom,' as Si was now known from Harriet Beecher Stowe's best-seller. The Queen was heavier than he recalled and wore black mourning clothes with her head covered in white lace. She invited Si to sign her guest book and expressed surprise at his 'hale and hearty looks, considering his great age.' She did not seem to recall having met him twenty-five years before at the Crystal Palace. She presented Henson with a photograph of herself mounted in a gold frame, signed *Victoria Reg. 1877*.

Although Henson was now 87, illustrations rendered at this time depict a white-bearded gentleman towering over a diminutive Queen Victoria, his head respectfully bowed.

The queen later wrote in her journal, 'Reading, in that most interesting book the Life of Mr. Josiah Henson, a fugitive slave and the original of Mrs. B. Stowe's *Uncle Tom's Cabin*. He is now in his 88th year, and his sufferings, energy, patient endurance, and his anxiety for the good of his suffering brethren, are admirable.'

Josiah enjoyed having the bumps and indentations upon his skull manipulated and analyzed by Professor Fowler, the famous phrenologist, who was then living in England. This means of determining a person's character and future promise was all the rage at this time.

"I supposed that my old slave master had beaten out

all my brains," Josiah told Fowler, laughing.

"Perhaps your skull was so thick those blows did not penetrate," the noted professor replied in all seriousness.

The Hensons sailed home from Liverpool on the 27th of April 1877 aboard the Cunard steamer *China*, bringing with them enough money to pay all the mortgages. They docked in Boston and returned home to Canada, remaining on the farm until the following winter.

Nancy was anxious to visit Baltimore where she grew up and to see her sister who still lived there, while Si had a hankering to see his boyhood home once more and visit his mother's grave. They stopped in Washington where Si showed Nancy the markets where he had delivered produce from Riley's farms so long ago.

They then made their way to the White House to pay a call on the nineteenth President of the United States, Rutherford B. Hayes. Si wished to meet the Chief Executive who had been a staunch abolitionist and continued to champion equal rights for blacks. Frederick Douglass arranged the meeting to gain this audience with President Hayes by sending his secretary a letter explaining 'this aged preacher is anxious to see the face of President Hayes if but for a minute.'

'I now hope for peace and what is more important, security and prosperity for the colored people,' Hayes wrote after serving in battle with the Union forces during the Civil War. The President was particularly interested in education for ex-slaves, 'to uplift the descendants of those who were thus oppressed.'

President Hayes and the First Lady greeted the Hensons warmly, and while Mrs. Hayes took Nancy on a tour through the famous mansion, (recently refurbished with a new piano, bathtubs with running water and a telephone), Si exchanged friendly conversation with the President. Henson chatted about his recent trip through England and praised the President for his former service as Governor of Ohio, the free state that had treated him so well when he was still a slave. Si and Nancy stayed for tea with the President and *Lemonade Lucy*, as Mrs. Hayes, a tee-totaler, was nicknamed in the press.

"Do call again," the President said cordially, "should you ever pay another visit to the Capital City."

Si and Nancy then hired a carriage and headed for Rockville, some twelve miles outside Washington.

Fifty years had passed since Si last set foot on the Maryland homestead where he'd been held in slavery. What hope he'd been filled with back then, his freedom papers stowed away in his knap-sack. The old place was shockingly run down. They passed through broken fences and dead orchards, shuddering at everything neglected and overgrown with brush and fallen trees. The barns and other outbuildings were gone, and the main house was dilapidated and in desperate need of paint.

"Do the Rileys still live here?" Si asked the African-

131

American boy who opened the creaking front door.

"Mistress Riley do." he nodded. "But she poorly. Not outa her bed today."

"Who is it, boy?" Si heard a woman's shaky voice call from inside.

"A black gentleman with his woman, ma'am."

There were no longer carpets on the floors, and the furniture was badly worn. Si hardly recognized Mathilda Riley, for she was still a vivacious twenty year old in Si's memory, while this thin invalid of seventy years lay stretched out on a chaise lounge. She stared at Si and Nancy blankly.

"Good day, Mistress Riley," said Si politely, stretching out his hand. "How are you?"

"Poorly, I be poorly," she replied. "How do you do?"

"I am very well, thank you," Si replied.

"I'm sorry. I don't seem to know you."

"It's Josiah Henson. Come to call with his wife, Nancy."

"Si!" she exclaimed. "How can it be? Come here and let me feel of your arms." She rose to her feet, and Si flung back his cloak so that she could put her trembling hands on his arms—the arms that had been shattered so long ago in her husband's defense.

"Why, it *is* you, Si! Land sakes! I cannot believe it!'"

"Indeed, 'tis me. You may believe it."

"After all these years!" Mistress Riley burst into tears. "Your master is dead and long gone, you know."

"Oh no, madam. My master is alive, for I am my

own master now."

"I mean Mister Riley, Si. Oh, if only he were here now, I know you would be good friends. I never blamed you for running away. Why, look at you! You're a gentleman!"

"I always was a gentleman, ma'am," said Si, standing tall.

Later the boy who'd let them in guided them to a small cemetery filled with wooden markers and crumbling stones. Among the many broken markers of slaves too soon departed, Si located the grave of his mother who had died during the time he first stayed with Amos Riley in Kentucky. As soon as Si spotted the crude wooden slab with Mama's name painted in crude letters, he fell to his knees and openly wept. Si longed to tell her how he'd managed to bring his brother, Jacob out of slavery into the Land of Liberty. Yet somehow, he thought she knew.

Epilogue

In the 1830s, Canada had not yet become a nation but consisted of six separate British colonies with a total population of less than three million, situated along the Great Lakes, the St. Laurence River, and the Atlantic Ocean. When the Henson family arrived, the area was known as the Province of Upper Canada. In 1841, it became the Province of Canada, and then in 1867, Ontario.

When Josiah Henson and his family arrived in 1830, there were but a few hundred fugitive slaves who had found their way here. By 1858, there were more than 35,000 (Bleby, p. 181).

According to Henson, 'In 1830, there were no schools among the Canadian fugitives and no churches. We now have numerous churches that are well-filled from Sabbath to Sabbath with attentive hearers. Our children attend the Sabbath School... We depend principal upon our own farms for subsistence, but some of our number are good mechanics, blacksmiths, carpenters, masons, shoemakers, and tailors. We find a ready market for all our products. The soil is fertile, and yields an abundant return for labor. Considerable attention is paid to the cultivation of fruit: apples, cherries, plums, peaches, quinces, currants, gooseberries, strawberries, etc. which will be very profitable in a few years. I have raised a delicious sweet potato on my farm as I ever saw in Kentucky and as good a crop of tobacco and hemp. The climate is good and the soil rich' (Bleby, p. 182).

Eager 'to help the government that gave us homes when we fled slavery,' Henson served with the 2nd Essex Company of Coloured Volunteers in the Canadian Militia during the Rebellion of 1837.

'Although I could not shoulder a musket, I could carry a sword,' he wrote. 'My company held Fort Malden six months and took the schooner *Ann* with its huge load of arms and munitions.'

Henson and his first wife, Charlotte, had twelve children of whom seven survived. Their eldest son, Tom, was in San Francisco at the outbreak of the American Civil War and enlisted on a man-o-war as soon as blacks were permitted to join the Union forces. Tom was never heard from again so it is believed he went down with his ship. Josiah Henson's son-in-law, Wheeler, enlisted in Detroit and also served in the Union Army during the Civil War.

Josiah and Charlotte's second son, Isaac, received

his formal education in London and was ordained a Methodist minister. He died at the age of 37.

Josiah Junior, who rode to freedom on his father's back, grew up to become a prosperous businessman in Michigan, while the youngest boy, Peter, remained at home in Dresden to manage the family farm.

Josiah and Nancy Henson had two daughters and a son. One daughter attended Oberlin College in Ohio.

Among the many who fled from slavery and found security in Canada was the humble friend who, at the beginning of their flight, put Josiah Henson and his family in a skiff and rowed them across the Ohio River. (Bleby, Henry, *Josiah: The Maimed Fugitive*. London, 1873, p. 157-158).

Henson preached his last sermon in April of 1883 at the age of 94. He collapsed three days later and died at Dresden on May 5, surrounded by his family. His final words were, 'I couldn't stay if I would, nor I wouldn't if I could' (Bordwich, Fergus M.. *Bound For Canaan: The Underground Railroad & the War for the Soul of America.* NY: Harper Collins/Amistad, 2005, p. 434).

In 1983, Josiah Henson became the first person of African American descent to be featured on a Canadian stamp. In 1999, Josiah Henson was recognized by the Historic Sites & Monuments Board of Canada as a National Historic Person.

Was Henson The Real 'Uncle Tom?'

In *A Key to Uncle Tom's Cabin, presenting the original Facts and Documents upon which the Story is Founded, Together with Corroborative Statements verifying the Truth of the Work* (Boston, MA: John P. Jewett & Co., 1853), author Harriet Beecher Stowe answered attacks from malicious critics who called her best seller 'a tissue of falsehoods,' with documented facts. In this book, Stowe paid tribute to 'the published memoirs of the venerable Josiah Henson, now pastor of the missionary settlement at Dawn in Canada.'

It was the editor John Lobb, who was chiefly responsible for Josiah Henson's identification as 'Uncle Tom,' since Stowe always claimed her title character represented a composite of ex-slaves whom she had met and interviewed over the years. She once related Henson to the George Harris character. However, due to the international fame of Stowe's novel, Josiah Henson became a sort of 19th century rock star and the most popular fugitive slave of his time.

Lobb revised and enlarged the third edition of Henson's autobiography entitling it *Uncle Tom's Story of His Life: An Autobiography of the Reverend Josiah Henson (Mrs. Harriet Beecher Stowe's 'Uncle Tom') From 1789 to 1876* (London, England, 1877; London, Ontario, 1881).

Unfortunately, in an era lacking protective copyright laws, and due to the seemingly endless *Tom Shows* or theatrical productions of Stowe's book, 'Uncle Tom' morphed from a man of quiet courage into a clueless, 'step-'n-fetch-it'; a rather pathetic fellow lacking backbone. Particularly after an essay published by author James Baldwin, this term developed highly negative implications, symbolizing any African American whose chief aim was to gain white approval and was therefore, considered a traitor to his race. The character of a black buffoon was certainly never Stowe's intention and Josiah Henson, if indeed, he actually did become the author's inspiration, was anything but meek and docile.

'People have forgotten that Mrs. Stowe's book is a novel. My name is not Tom and never was,' Henson claimed on more than one occasion. 'I do not want to have any other name inserted in the newspapers for me than my own: *Josiah Henson*… always was and always will be.

I believe her book to be the beginning of the glorious end of slavery,' he said. According to Si, 'It was the wedge that finally rent asunder that gigantic fabric with a fearful crash.'

In 1879 at the age of 80, Henson said, 'Since 1852, I have been called 'Uncle Tom,' and I feel proud of the title. If my humble words in any way inspired that gifted lady to write such a plaintive story that the whole community has been touched with pity for the sufferings of the poor slave, then I have not lived in vain. Though Mrs. Stowe made her hero die, it was fit she did this to complete her story. If God had not given to me a giant's strength I should have died over and over again myself long before I reached Canada. I regard it as one of the most remarkable features of my life that I have rallied after so many exposures to all kinds of hardships.'

According to Josiah Henson, 'Mrs. Stowe's book is not an exaggerated account of the evils of slavery. The truth has never been half told for that story would be too horrible to hear…'

About Juliet Mofford

Juliet Mofford earned a degree from Tufts University and pursued graduate studies in art history at Boston University and in Europe. She has lived in eleven states and six foreign countries. Before embarking upon a career as a professional museum educator, she taught English language and American culture in Japan, Spain, and Puerto Rico.

Under MA Cultural Council Grants, Mofford wrote and produced two plays based on the 1692 Salem Witch Trials, *Cry Witch!* and *The Suspicious Season.* She served as project director for three Maine Humanities Council grants and a National Endowment for the Humanities Youth Pilot Grant that enabled high school students to research, write, perform, and film an original historical play for the community.

Mofford represented New England on the Educational Board of the American Association of Museums and in 2005, received a Preservation Award from the Town of Andover and Andover Historic Preservation Commission.

Two of Mofford's twelve published books received national awards from the American Association for State & Local History. She has been a reviewer for *Scholastic Teacher Magazine*, evaluating classroom materials and writing educational features on assignment. Her articles have appeared in the *New York Times*, *Boston Globe*, *Christian Science Monitor*, *Miami Herald*, *Chicago Tribune*, *Montreal Gazette*, *Travel/Holiday*, *Museum Magazine*, *Caribbean Beachcomber*, *Antiques Week*, *Young World*, and *American History Illustrated*. Mofford's article "Josiah Henson: The Slave Who Inspired a Best Seller" was published in *Learning Through History* in February 2009.

Mofford directed Teacher Training Workshops and taught courses on slavery for the Essex Heritage organization, Middlesex College, and Northern Essex Community College. While Director of Education and Research at Andover Historical Society, she produced a traveling exhibit on slavery, which is when she discovered Josiah Henson and his connection with author Harriet Beecher Stowe, an Andover resident from 1853 until 1864.

The mother of three adult children, Juliet Mofford lives in mid-coast Maine, where she works as a full-time writer and historical researcher.

Sources

It is important to note that this book has been chiefly drawn from Henson's own three slave narratives.

The three autobiographies by Josiah Henson opened the eyes of many people at the time to the tragedy and cruelty of slavery. Slave Narratives or personal stories told by former slaves of their lives and experiences in bondage, represented a popular genre during the late eighteenth and nineteenth centuries, particularly among those with anti-slavery sympathies. Such autobiographies and pamphlets were generally promoted and published through the efforts of dedicated abolitionists. Most were *as told to* stories by African Americans to white interviewers, who also wrote the introductions and prefaces, acted as editors, and promoted wide circulation and sales. These tales of suffering, often including dramatic escapes to freedom, Christian redemption, and happy endings, strongly influenced public attitudes towards anti-slavery. Frederick Douglass, author of one of the first and most powerful slave narratives, believed it was the responsibility of free blacks to share their experiences and educate the public regarding the horrors of slavery. The different editions of Josiah Henson's autobiographies are unique in that the author and central character used his slave narratives as fundraisers.

BLEBY, Henry. *Josiah: The Maimed Fugitive*. London, 1873.

BORDWICH, Fergus M. *Bound For Canaan: The Underground Railroad & the War for the Soul of America*. NY: Harper Collins/Amistad, 2005.

LOBB, John. *The Young People's Illustrated Edition of Uncle Tom's Story of His Life* (from 1789 to 1877. London, England, 1877. – John Lobb also released enlarged and revised editions in 1876, 1881, and 1890. Harriet Beecher Stowe wrote a preface to the 1881 edition but made no mention of Henson having served as inspiration for her 'Uncle Tom' character. This enlarged edition of Henson's autobiography was published in London, Ontario: Schuler, Smith and Company.

MOFFORD, Juliet Haines. "Josiah Henson: The Slave Who Inspired a Best Seller." *Learning Through History Magazine*, February 2009, pp. 47-50.

NORTH American Slave Narratives, University of North Carolina, Chapel Hill:
docsouth.unc.edu/neh/henson58/menu.html
docsouth.unc.edu/neh/henson49/henson49.html
digitalhistory.uh.edu/black_voices/voices_display.cfm?id

THE Life of Josiah Henson, formerly a Slave, Now an Inhabitant of Canada, Narrated by Himself (perhaps ghost—written by Samuel A. Eliot.). Arthur D. Phelps: Boston, MA, 1849. London, England & Edinburgh, Scotland, 1851.

TRUTH Stranger Than Fiction: Father Henson's Story of His Own Life, with revisions by John Lobb. Boston, MA: John P. Jewett, 1858; London, 1859.

TRUTH Stranger Than Fiction: An Autobiography of the Reverend Josiah Henson (Mrs. Harriet Beecher Stowe's "Uncle Tom") from 1789 to 1879, with preface by Mrs. Stowe, introductory notes by Wendell Phillips, John Greenleaf Whittier, George Sturge & Samuel Morley, Esq. & appendix by Gilbert Haven. Boston, MA; London, Ontario: John Lobb, editor, 1878.

Henson Sites To Visit

Now owned by the Maryland National Capital Park and Planning Commission, **Uncle Tom's Cabin**, located off Old Georgetown Road in Bethesda, Montgomery County, Maryland, opened to the public in 2006. The slave cabin where Josiah Henson slept from 1795 to 1830, working on Isaac Riley's 3,700-acre plantation, no longer exists. This mid-nineteenth century structure of oak beams is still covered with bark but has hardwood floors. When a dozen men, women, and children held as slaves lived here, the floors were simply dirt.

The Search for Josiah Henson, an archaeology dig on Issac Riley's farm in Maryland. PBS, 2014. Visit: http://www.pbs.org/video/2365243972

Uncle Tom's Cabin Museum Historic Site is located on Uncle Tom's Road, R.R. #5 in Dresden, Ontario. Occupying five of the original 200 acres purchased in the mid-nineteenth century to start the

British American Institute, it is an hour and a half north of Detroit, Michigan. Established as a museum in 1948 and acquired by Ontario Heritage Trust in 2005, the historic site is open daily from Victoria Day (the Monday preceding May 25) through mid-October.

The last home lived in by Henson and his family can be found here. Constructed of cedar and tulipwood, this two-story clapboard house represents a substantial one for rural Ontario in the mid-nineteenth century. Visitors can tour the **Henson Family Cemetery** and several heritage structures including the **Harris House**, one of the area's oldest buildings and a final stop on the **Underground Railroad**. The site also encompasses a sawmill, smokehouse, and a pioneer church with the pulpit from the original church where Henson preached in Dresden. **The Josiah Henson Interpretive Center and Museum** contains books and artifacts from the slave era, related to abolition, the Underground Railroad and Henson's life.

Visit: www.uncletomscabin.org

Images

Images on the following pages are in the public domain with the exception of the final two, which were provided courtesy of Steven Cook, Director of the Josiah Henson Historical Site at Dresden in Ontario.

Josiah Henson, younger years

Josiah Henson

Josiah Henson

Henson Family Arrives in Canada

Henson

Henson

Portrait drawing of United States-born Canadian
abolitionist and writer Josiah Henson

Nancy and Josiah Henson

Josiah Henson and unknown white male

Queen Victoria and Rev. Josiah Henson

THE

LIFE OF JOSIAH HENSON,

FORMERLY A SLAVE,

NOW AN INHABITANT OF CANADA,

AS

NARRATED BY HIMSELF.

BOSTON:
ARTHUR D. PHELPS.
1849.

Underground Routes to Canada

Henson House, 2011

Uncle Tom's Cabin

Index

Made in the USA
Las Vegas, NV
19 February 2024

85942607R00095